WET and FAT

Jon Lien, Leesa Fawcett, Sue Staniforth

Memorial University of Newfoundland

Drawings by Don Wright

BREAKWATER

WET and FAT

Whales and Seals of Newfoundland and Labrador

WRIGHT '82

Canadian Cataloguing in Publication Data

Lien, Jon, 1939-
    Wet and fat : whales and seals of Newfoundland
and Labrador

ISBN 0-919519-76-8

1. Whales — Newfoundland — Identification.
2. Whales — Newfoundland — Labrador — Identification.
3. Seals (Animals) — Newfoundland — Identification.
4. Seals (Animals) — Newfoundland — Labrador —
Identification. I. Fawcett, Leesa. II. Staniforth,
Sue. III. Title.

QL737.C4L53 1985   599.5'09718   C85-098793-8

CAUTION

The Whale Research Group of Memorial University was set
up in 1978 in response to the ecological, economic and social
problems brought about by the entrapment of whales in
inshore fishing gear. The research of the group has remained
focussed on trying to elucidate the effects of this interaction.
However, activities have diversified to include studies of the
behaviour, equality, and population dynamics of whales,
the incidence of shark entrapment in fishing gear and
educating Newfoundlanders about their marine
environment.

Although based in the Newfoundland/Labrador
region, the Whale Research Group has undertaken research
off West Greenland, the Indian Ocean, Norway and off the
Galapogos Islands.

● ● ●

Don Wright is an artist living in a Newfoundland fishing
community, whose work has long been involved with the
coastal environment.

For several years he has worked closely with Jon Lien
of the Whale Research Group, Memorial University, as
designer and illustrator of a series of posters and educational
material concerning marine life.

His prints and drawings are in many national
collections including the National Gallery of Canada and
the Canada Council Art Bank.

TABLE OF CONTENTS

Introducing Whales

There are 80 or so species of cetacea including whales, dolphins, and porpoises in the world. There are 34 species of pinnipeds which include seals, sea-lions, fur seals and walrus. About 17 species of whales, dolphins, and porpoises can be seen in Newfoundland and Labrador waters. Six species of seals and walrus occur here. These marine mammals are some of the most impressive and fascinating animals in our waters. This book was written to help you recognize the common species seen in Newfoundland and Labrador, and to provide some basic information on each.

There is good reason to include whales and seals in the same book. Biologically, they show similar adaptations, as both groups have evolved to live in a marine environment. While wet refers to their ecological situation, fat refers to their typical adaptation to feeding and temperature conditions.

Whales and seals, like ourselves, are air-breathing, warm-blooded animals, who bear live young and nurse them on milk. Unlike most other mammals, whales and seals have adapted specifically to an aquatic lifestyle. They are relatively large, have a thick fat layer under the skin, and are streamlined for movement through the water. Their large size is vital for reducing heat loss in cold water and also gives them added swimming power. The blubber acts as a food reserve and helps with insulation and buoyancy. By reducing the extent and number of limbs, and by rounding out their contours, whales and seals also minimize heat loss and become more streamlined in the water.

The province of Newfoundland and Labrador is one of the best places in the world to see many species of seals and whales. Some of the species commonly seen here are infrequently viewed in other areas. For other species, such as the harp seal, the humpback whale, and the white-beaked dolphin, the province has been the focus of world attention.

Whales live entirely in the sea and are helpless on land. Their young are born in the water and must swim immediately to the surface for their first breath of air. Seals on the other hand, have not totally forsaken land. Seals come to land or ice to birth their young, to moult their coats or just to haul-out and rest; their remaining time is spent in the water. This dual lifestyle makes it necessary for the seal to adapt to both water and land.

This guide is designed to make identification of whales and seals as easy as possible by pointing out key features of the species you could encounter. Once you have identified an animal, you may want to find out more about it. Along with identification information, the distribution, abundance, and natural history of each species are described, and local stories and accounts are given.

Whale-watching — What to Do and Where to Go

All you need to identify whales are a field guide, a good set of rain gear, lots of patience, and a bit of luck. Whale-watching is challenging; different whales are frequently difficult to tell apart, and often only a small part of the animal can be glimpsed for a second or two. Conditions under which whales are seen vary greatly; visibility, sea state, distance and duration of the sighting all affect how much information you have to determine the species. As in bird-watching, it helps to know field marks of the various species. With practice and patience, it's possible for anyone to become an expert whale-watcher.

opposite - Humpback whale breaching

Good binoculars, telescopes, and telephoto lenses come in handy, especially when sighting from shore.

The first trace of a whale is usually the very small, far-off puff of a spout on the horizon. Groups of seabirds may catch your attention first, circling over the feeding whales and diving for bait. Keep your eyes focused on the general area of that last puff of spray; odds are the whale will blow again in that vicinity. Your next view might be of a dorsal fin atop a smooth, glistening back. Keep on watching!

A key feature to notice when you sight a whale is its size; is it a large animal (over 30 feet/9m), a medium-sized animal (18-30 feet/5-9m), or a small animal (under 18 feet/5m)? This may be difficult to decide at first, due to visibility and distance, but usually a rough estimate can be made by comparing the whale to waves, fishing boats, or points of land in the area.

Other features to notice include: colour and shape; the shape of the blow and the appearance of the blow relative to sighting the back, dorsal fin, and tail flukes; and the shape of the dorsal fin, if present. Note if the animal is alone or in a group and try and determine its diving and blowing pattern. This may seem like a lot to look for.

In this guide we've divided up the whales first with respect to size - the large, medium, and small whale sections. The beginning of each section presents a list of species in that group, and key information you need to discriminate between species. When you have an idea of the whale you've sighted, turn to the section on that species for more detailed information.

Don't worry if at first you have trouble judging size. If you're not sure, for instance, that the whale sighted is medium or small, look under both sections. With practice the task will become quite easy.

Newfoundland and Labrador waters change considerably at different times of the year. Species abundance also varies by location.

When whales die they frequently float and drift to land where they are occasionally found on beaches. A dead whale, because of decomposition, appears quite different from a live whale. To aid in identifying any stranded specimens you may encounter, there is a special section for each species which gives you critical points to check.

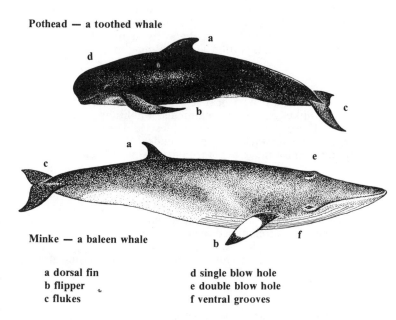

Pothead — a toothed whale

Minke — a baleen whale

a dorsal fin
b flipper
c flukes

d single blow hole
e double blow hole
f ventral grooves

Some Do's and Don'ts for Whale Watchers

Watching whales can be exhilarating and educational, but it is important that neither whales nor whale-watchers be disturbed or harmed. Whales are fascinating creatures to observe, yet remember that they are also huge wild animals, and so must be treated with respect. Regulations under the Fisheries Act forbid harassment of whales, dolphins, and porpoises.

Never chase whales in a boat, or split up groups of animals, particularly mothers and calves. Propeller blades can injure whales, and boats that veer too closely could disrupt feeding and resting activities. Whales can also cause a lot of damage to a boat!

Maintain a respectful distance from whales at least 150 feet (50 metres). Let the animal come closer to you if it is curious and wishes to investigate. Remember whales are wild animals; give them time to get use to your presence.

Always leave your engine idling slowly, even when you are stationary. This lets the whale know where you are at all times. Ocassional incidents of whales colliding with or breaching onto boats seem to have been the result of boats drifting silently, giving the whale no audible clues to it's whereabouts.

Move slowly towards and away from the animals, avoiding sudden changes in speed or direction.

Steer clear of fishing gear while on the water. Any excess activity could scare fish away from the area, and motors easily snag on mooring lines and nets. Disturbing whales around fishing gear could cause them to panic and blunder into the gear, causing much damage to the nets and often injuring or drowning the animal.

Scuba Divers: Do not dive in the vicinity of whale activity, especially lunge-feeding or breaching whales. Romantic notions of playfully hitching a ride on whales' dorsal fins could lead to serious injury.

Onshore: There are many excellent locations for watching whales from land throughout Newfoundland and Labrador. Some of these are listed at the back of the book. High cliffs and coastal headlands which overlook deep water are excellent sites, especially when inshore populations of bait such as capelin and squid are abundant.

Ask any fisherman in your area; he'll know if bait species are plentiful and if whales are around. He'll probably be able to recommend good vantage points as well. Fishermen are always the best local experts on where and when to find whales.

Humpback whale's flukes

9

WRIGHT '82

Whale Strandings

Many different kinds of whales strand. In Newfoundland, pothead whales mass strand most commonly, but there have been cases of sperm whales and white-sided dolphins stranding. Mass strandings seem to be unique to offshore, toothed-whale species. In recent years, pothead strandings have occurred at Point au Gaul, Point Leamington, and Grand Beach, and have involved hundreds of animals.

Facts About Mass Strandings

Although several theories have been proposed, no one really knows why mass strandings occur. There may be a different explanation for each stranding. Strandings should be viewed as accidents, due to internal problems or external circumstances, with many factors probably contributing to their cause. The theories that have been put forth can be divided into two categories.

Internally-caused strandings may be due to the effects of illness or parasites, resulting in a loss of the animal's directional sense. It has also been proposed that one animal (perhaps a group "leader") may become sick or confused and lead the whole herd ashore.

Externally-caused strandings may involve environmental factors such as pollution, the characteristics of shoaling beaches, or the presence of a predator. Recent findings also suggest that mass strandings occur in areas where there are geomagnetic anomalies.

The fact that mass-stranded whales often come back to shore when towed off makes it tempting to consider these events a kind of "mass suicide". However, some whales have been successfully towed offshore, while others have refloated themselves on the next high tide after their stranding and stayed offshore. It is doubtful that mass suicides are a typical characteristic of whales or any other animal, since such behaviour is biologically unadaptive and reduces a species' chances of survival in the long run.

So far, no single theory exists which can explain mass strandings. Hopefully, by studying each stranding situation, we will someday understand why these mysterious events occur.

Strandings offer valuable opportunities for people to learn more about whales. Each animal is studied both internally and externally, in order to gain as much information as possible. If the animals are dead, scientists begin a careful study of each individual and its relationship to other animals. First, each whale is numbered, measured, and sexed. It is then examined for any external wounds, scars, or parasites, and the thickness of its blubber is measured. Then the animal is examined internally. Females are checked to see if they are producing milk, or are pregnant. All animals are examined for parasites and disease. Often, tissue samples are taken for later analysis. Such analysis provides basic information on the biology and physiology of the animal. As toothed whales can be aged by examining their teeth in a lab, the lower jaws are cut off each animal.

Often, parts of the whale are photographed, such as the pattern found on a pothead's belly. This pattern can be compared to the pattern found on potheads in other parts of the world. In general, scientists try and gather as much information as possible from each stranded whale.

opposite — Pothead whales mass stranding at Point au Gaul, July 1979

What to Do: General

If whales, dolphins, or seals are found washed up on a beach in your area, or if whales mass-strand, there are several things you can do to alert scientists, gather information, and aid live animals. Please call the Whale Research Group at Memorial University, 753-5495, day or night. We accept collect calls, and if we are not in, a recorder will tape your message. Notify the nearest office of the Department of Fisheries and Oceans as well.

Local observers can help by recording:
(1) When the animals were found
(2) Weather at the time of stranding
(3) Description of the animals
(4) Description of the stranding site
(5) Number of animals stranded and their condition
(6) Number of animals in the area (any seen swimming in the bay or offshore)
(7) Accessibility of stranding site (near a road, or village, or on a remote beach)
(8) Names and phone numbers of people involved

Remember that stranded animals are still wild animals. When helpless or injured, the close activity of man may seriously stress the animal.

Live Animals

Seals that come to shore and are unable or unwilling to return to sea when approached are usually injured or sick. The best treatment is to leave them alone until help arrives. Noise, crowding, and unnecessary handling should be avoided. Approach a seal cautiously, and keep away from the mouth. They are quick and can bite.

Large whales can be very difficult to work with when they are stranded alive. Any whale will over-heat in the air, so pouring water on them or maintaining a covering of wet rags or towels on their exposed bodies and shading them from the sun will help prevent this. Covering the eyes may help keep the animal calm. Crowds and noise should be avoided if possible. Stay well back for safety. At times stranded animals may thrash violently.

In 1979, fishermen at Point au Gaul were successful in saving over 30 whales by towing them off the beach. The only practical method of returning a large whale to sea is carefully towing it by the tail. The line should be non-abrasive (braided nylon is best) and tied around the flukes with a loop wide enough that it can be shed if the whale escapes before the line is removed. Although most stranded animals simply restrand when towed from the beach, sometimes they can be successfully rescued in this way.

Dead Animals

Dead animals should be reported as well, as they are a valuable source of information.

Dead marine mammals smell horrible. Depending on the condition of the animals, and if they are near a community, immediate disposal may be the next step. The town council or the provincial Department of Environment will usually assist in cleaning up after a stranding.

Burial at or near the stranding site is the best solution. Towing an animal out to sea often results in the carcass being washed up elsewhere, or tangling in fishing gear. Attempts to burn or detonate carcasses have been singularly unsuccessful.

Whaling in Newfoundland

There is a good deal of literature on whaling, including the history and technology of the hunt, the economics of whale products, plus stories, songs and legends revolving around this ancient occupation. Most Newfoundlanders remember the 1960s drive fisheries for pothead whales. Still, whaling in Newfoundland and Labrador began long before that.

Off the coast of Labrador the Inuit have been hunting whales for centuries. They originally hunted from large kayaks (25-30 ft./7-9 m long) containing up to 8 men, who used ivory harpoons with iron tips. Today native·Canadians are still allowed to kill small numbers of whales, solely for local use and not for commercial purposes.

The first to visit our waters in search of whales were the Basques (from the Bay of Biscay) in the 16th century. The first Spaniard to visit the Grand Banks was a sailor, Matias de Echeveste who made 28 voyages to Newfoundland from 1545-1599. Archeologists are now studying a Basque whaling station that was unearthed at Red Bay, Labrador. English, Norwegian and American whalers came during the late 1800s and early 1900s. With modern whaling came the invention of the exploding harpoon and the construction of floating factory ships and shore station factories to process the whales.

The Newfoundland Whaling Company was formed in 1900. In 1905 there were 18 whaling stations in operation around the province. (See page 8: Map of Whaling Stations). With the acceleration of whaling local concern over the activity increased. By 1950 there were only 3 active whaling stations left: at Williamsport (White Bay), Hawke's Harbour (Labrador) and Dildo (Trinity Bay). Whales were becoming scarce.

In the 1960s the International Whaling Commission (established in Washington in 1946) set strict quotas on the number of whales that could be taken. In 1972 Canada banned commercial whaling. There is still limited hunting of whales today. Quotas are set on each species and whalers are forbidden to hunt any species which is endangered. Such restriction on harvesting should allow populations of whales to increase. The I.W.C. passed a resolution for all commercial whaling to cease by 1986, but so far Japan, Norway and the U.S.S.R. have not agreed to it.

A great deal of our knowledge of whale anatomy and biology comes from research done during whaling times at the shore stations. Frederick True of the New York Museum worked out of St. John's while compiling his classic 1904 study, 'The Whalebone Whales of the Western North Atlantic.'

Canada withdrew from the International Whaling Commission in 1981 and announced it had no commercial interests in whaling. Canada's native whaling is monitored by the Ministers Commission on Whales and Whaling which reports to the Federal Minister of Fisheries and Oceans.

Thar She Blows

Whaling required not only skill and experience but a knowledge of the whale's behaviour and habits. There were several enlightened whaling captains who proved to be excellent marine biologists and naturalists.

One such man is Captain Henry Mahle, a Newfoundlander who lives in Dildo, Trinity Bay. Captain Mahle was born in Norway where whaling was a highly organized, multi-million dollar business. He was actively engaged in whaling until 1972 and is one of the last Newfoundland whalers. At times Henry likes to talk about the time he spent as a whaler.

"Whaling was a part of fishing. I started off on a whale catcher as a deckhand, then became a mate and eventually a gunner and a skipper."

"You kind of develop a skill for finding the plankton — the feed of the whales. Once we found a whale we'd determine which way it was moving. We called it tracking. Before the faster boats came along, in the slower boats, we had to sneak up and outsmart the whale.

"Whaling here in Dildo was mostly geared for small whales — minkes and potheads. We had pretty small boats — 45 feet (15 metres) that's what we had here. The guns for small whales were 50 mm and the 90 mm was for the bigger whales. Finbacks were the hardest to catch and humpbacks were the easiest.

"There were many little tricks. If you could see a humpback you'd circle around him quickly in your boat. That would lay down a curtain of bubbles, like a corral. Nine out of ten times he'd come up within that circle."

"Minke whales are harder to shoot than the big whales. They are fast and small and zig-zag all over the place. They are so quick! Minkes will jump clear out of the water sometimes. They used all the minke meat - called it Arctic steak or Japanese bacon. Minke whale tastes like a T-bone steak. Most of our production was shipped to Norway and there was a Norwegian and a Japanese grader here in Dildo."

"We respected the whales we hunted. We respected a female with her calf. We never shot one like that, but we were out to make a living too."

Location of Whaling Stations in Newfoundland and Labrador

Whale Watching Locations

Land Lookouts

Cape St. Mary's: lighthouse overlooking Placentia Bay
St.Mary's Bay: beach at St. Vincents and surrounding cliffs
Cape Race
Witless Bay: around seabird sanctuary
Cape Spear: lighthouse
Cape St. Francis: lighthouse
Signal Hill, St. John's
Holyrood Arm, Conception Bay: good for potheads when there is squid
Fortune Bay: from Grand Bank, Point May
Argentia
Bay de Verde: cliffs
Terra Nova Park: Newman Sound, Eastport, Happy Adventure
Bonavista Bay: Salvage, Elliston
Trinity Bay: Trinity, Cape Bonavista
New World Island
Strait of Belle Isle
White Bay
Bay of Islands
Labrador: Groswater Bay, Bay of Islands

Ferries

Conception Bay: aboard Bell Island ferry
Hamilton Sound: aboard Fogo Island ferry
Argentia: ferry crossing to North Sydney, Nova Scotia
South Coast: coastal boat, especially early summer
Gulf of St. Lawrence: aboard ferry from Nova Scotia
Fortune Bay: aboard ferry to St. Pierre et Miquelon
Labrador: aboard coastal ferry from Lewisport and St. Anthony

Whale and Seabird Associations

Newfoundland and Labrador has one of the largest seabird populations in the world. Our offshore waters are rich fishing grounds that attract between 35-45 million birds a year! There are over twenty major breeding colonies for seabirds in Newfoundland and Labrador, such as Witless Bay, Baccalieu Island and Funk Island. The productive fishing grounds that attract birds also attract marine mammals. To describe the seabirds of Newfoundland and Labrador in any detail would require another entire field guide, but we can take a look at the interactions of whales and seabirds.

Even if you don't see any whales on an excursion, you are bound to observe some form of marine bird life. Groups of circling seabirds may also be your first clue that whales are in an area. Both marine birds and mammals are attracted by the presence of schooling bait, such as capelin or squid. Plunge-diving gannets, or swarms of raucous gulls can be seen and often heard over long distances; aim your boat or binoculars in their general direction and watch closely!

Whale and seabird associations are very well known, and have been recognized for centuries. Whalers would use feeding seabirds as a clue to the presence of whales. Fishermen also use whale and seabird feeding activity as an indicator of where to set their nets.

All the observed interactions between different seabirds and cetaceans are probably due to the presence of shared prey. However, some species are seen together more often than others. Both diet requirements and feeding methods may be important factors in these associations.

In the North Atlantic, humpbacks, minkes, pothead whales, and common dolphins are most often recorded with one or more seabird species.

Humpback whales feed primarily on capelin off Newfoundland and Labrador. Groups of whales often herd the fish into tight schools and then lunge towards them, through the surface of the water pushing fish ahead of them. Gulls and shearwaters can often be seen diving for leftovers as humpbacks lunge-feed. Puffins, guillemots, and auks feed by making relatively deep dives from the surface. They too can be seen feeding on capelin in the same areas as humpbacks. Sometimes when whales are lunge-feeding, seabirds are accidentally swallowed with the gulps of fish.

Minke whales often feed by driving fish to the surface from deeper waters. This brings them within range of surface-feeding birds, such as kittiwakes, terns, gulls, shearwaters, and petrels, which are usually recorded with feeding minkes.

Pothead whales and common dolphins also feed by herding schools of bait into tight concentrations. This makes the prey more accessible to diving birds such as gannets, murres, puffins, and guillemots. Dolphins often breach during feeding, which may be used partially to herd or stun fish. This breaching activity may also attract seabirds to the feeding sites. Scavenging gulls and shearwaters can be seen taking stunned and injured fish left by the dolphins.

Whale faeces are another food source for surface-feeding seabirds and scavengers. Petrels and pothead whales are often associated in this manner.

Other North Atlantic species such as blues, finbacks, orcas, and sperm whales are not as regularly associated with seabirds. These whales use different feeding methods and/or prey on bait species which are not as useful to seabirds. However, killer whales have been known to eat seabirds; a different type of interaction altogether!

Who benefits from these associations? It seems to be mostly the seabirds. Whales feeding at the surface in an area provide visual clues to birds of the presence of a relatively unpredictable and patchily distributed food supply. Whales that lunge-feed, or concentrate bait at the surface seem to provide an opportunity for birds to feed more easily.

However, some researchers say whales may also benefit, by using feeding seabirds as a prey indicator. Gannets and kittiwakes are the seabirds most commonly associated with whale species. It is interesting to note that they are both white birds, and easily visible at a distance. Many whale species spy-hop when far out at sea, and plunge diving gannets, or swarms of feeding kittiwakes could serve as possible clues to a prospective meal.

Whatever the causes, accidental or intentional, whale - seabird interactions are a fascinating part of whale-watching. So bring along a bird field guide too, and enjoy the birds.

opposite — **Minke whales and kittiwakes feeding on capelin in the cove at Port Kirwan**

Whales of Newfoundland and Labrador

Food Guide

Within the natural history notes for each of the individual whale and seal species, you will find pictorial representations of the food most commonly associated with that species. On this page is the complete labelled guide to all of the food pictures in the book. Keep in mind that they represent only the *most common* food for each of the species.

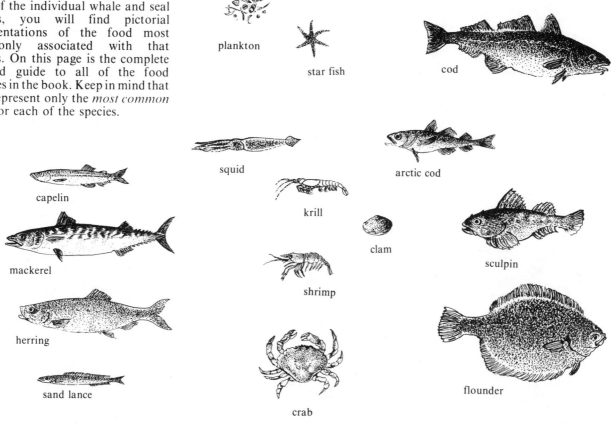

plankton

star fish

cod

squid

arctic cod

capelin

krill

clam

sculpin

mackerel

shrimp

herring

sand lance

crab

flounder

Drawings not to scale

Large Whales

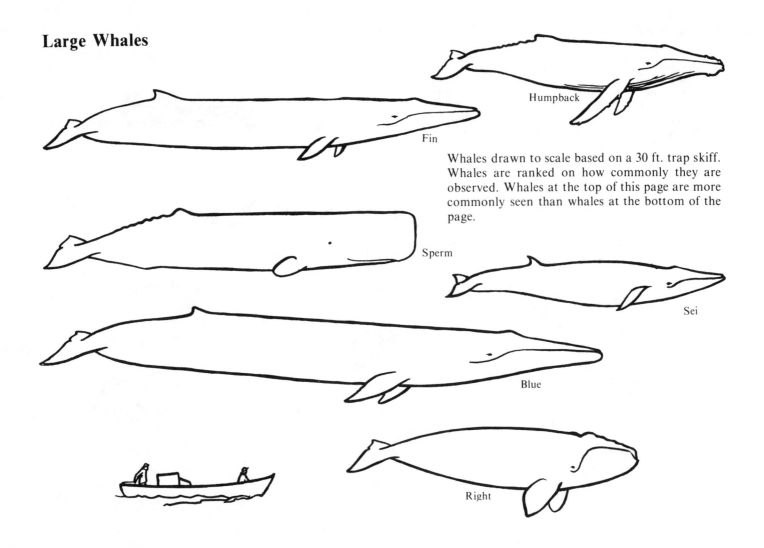

Humpback

Fin

Whales drawn to scale based on a 30 ft. trap skiff. Whales are ranked on how commonly they are observed. Whales at the top of this page are more commonly seen than whales at the bottom of the page.

Sperm

Sei

Blue

Right

Key information in identifying large whales

	Humpback	Fin	Sei	Blue	Sperm	Right
Shape of Blow						
Dorsal fins						
Flukes on Dive		Not visible	Not visible			

Humpback surfaces next to fishermen hauling a cod trap

Humpback Whale *(Megaptera novaeangliae)*

Common names: Hump, Trouble, Keporkak

Identification

- commonly seen inshore in summer especially when capelin abundant
- most sightings from May-September — some winter sightings
- usually seen singly, or in small loose groups (2-8 animals)
- 35-40 ft. (11-13m) long — young animals from 25 ft. (8m)
- most notable are the long, white flippers about one third of the body length
- robust body with broad, rounded head
- wart-like kobs on the head distinguishable at close range
- baleen is dark
- back is black — undersides are mostly white
- dorsal fin located about two-thirds of the way back is variable in shape
- frequently the dorsal fin appears to be on a hump — conspicuous when diving
- blow bushy, balloon-shaped — often seen first — then the back
- after a series of 5-10 blows — a terminal dive sometimes occurs
- on most terminal dives the tail flukes can be seen clearly above water
- fluke pattern can be used to identify individuals like finger prints
- may be seen lunge feeding, breaching, flippering or lob-tailing

Identification of stranded animals

- most positive trait is the presence of the long flippers
- look for knobs on head, dark brown or black baleen
- very large soft tongue may be extending from mouth
- 14-22 ventral grooves extending to navel

Distribution and Abundance

Humpbacks usually make coastal migrations, between cold water feeding grounds in summer, and tropical breeding grounds in winter. They occur in all oceans in both hemispheres. In the northwest Atlantic, humpbacks are found off the West Indies in winter, and near Bermuda in the spring. There are infrequent winter sightings of humpbacks around Newfoundland, particularly in Trinity Bay. Most animals start returning to Newfoundland in April and are seen first on the south coast. In summer, humpbacks are seen in inshore and offshore waters off Newfoundland and Labrador. Sightings near shore around the Avalon Peninsula, and on the northeast coast are common, especially from June to August. Sightings decrease in August. In the fall, probably by late October, most humpbacks have moved offshore and headed south.

Because of long pregnancy and weaning periods, humpback populations are slow to multiply, and whaling quickly depleted their numbers. In 1955 whaling for this species ended world-wide.

At that time the northwest Atlantic population was estimated to be below 1,000 animals. The present Northwest Atlantic population is about 3,000 to 4,000 and humpbacks are thus still considered an endangered species.

Natural History

Born in the Caribbean, a humpback is about 16 ft. (5m) long and weighs 2 tons (1800 kg). When weaned about 11 months later, it will be 25-28 ft. (8-9m) long. At about 35 ft. (11m), it is sexually mature and weighs 30-40 tons (27-36000 kg). On attaining maturity, a female usually calves about every two years, although in some cases a female may produce a calf each year. A typical lifespan for a humpback is approximately 30 years.

The humpback feeds in northern waters in the summer, and then migrates south to mate and calve during winter months. During the winter they do not feed. When breeding, male humpbacks make long, beautiful, complicated vocalizations. These songs probably have a role in the breeding process.

Humpbacks also produce a variety of social vocalizations in addition to songs. While in Newfoundland and Labrador waters they only produce social vocalizations and do not sing. These sounds are low frequency calls that sound a bit like those of a domestic pig.

For reasons which are poorly understood, humpbacks engage in a variety of behaviours which are commonly seen near shore. They may breach, driving their entire body from the water into the air. Sometimes, they lie on their sides and roll, waving their huge white flippers in the air, slapping the water, and sometimes each other with them. Humpbacks will also lobtail; lifting their flukes high into the air and repeatedly striking the surface of the water. These spectacular acrobatics make for great whale-watching! They may also provide the basis for the story of how the swordfish and the thresher shark kill whales.

opposite — **Humpbacks flippering**

The Legend of the
Swordfish - Thresher Shark

This legend has been told throughout the centuries by seafarers from around the world, and is still alive in Newfoundland and Labrador. It tells of wild battles that occur when the swordfish and the thresher shark attack the whale.

Some reports say that sharks and swordfish are confused with killer whales, which do occasionally attack other whales. Thresher sharks have enormously long tails, which they use to herd and stun schools of fish. However, they eat primarily mackerel and herring, and don't have the teeth or jaws to go after larger prey. The slapping of the humpback's long flippers could be mistaken for the lashing action of the thresher's long tail.

Accounts of swordfish attacking whales are rare, although several fragments of swordfish "swords" have been found embedded in the flanks of many whales taken by the whaling industry.

However, an account of two different animals cooperating to attack a third is a rare biological phenomenon. These strange tales are probably the result of mistaken observations of frolicking humpback whales. Humpbacks are well known for their antics, but the biological function of these behaviours is not known.

Humpback Feeding

Collisions with Fishing Gear

In Newfoundland, humpbacks feed on capelin, krill, sand lance and squid. Their primary food is capelin. Offshore, such as on the Southeast Shoal and Hamilton Bank, and inshore locations where capelin density is high are likely sighting areas.

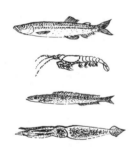

From 1977-1980, humpbacks appeared inshore in greater numbers than had previously been observed or have been observed since. During this period they frequently collided with fishing gear. These collisions resulted in serious losses to fishermen (up to 2.5 million dollars in 1979) and frequently entrapped the whale in fishing gear. This inshore increase in numbers of humpbacks coincided with depleted capelin stocks and increased inshore fishing effort. From 1980-83, damages decreased and humpbacks caused less trouble for fishermen. A program operated by Fisheries and Oceans Canada and Memorial University now aids fishermen with entrapped whales to minimize gear damage and insure safe release of the animals.

Although the humpback is considered a pest to fishermen, many fishermen have cooperated well with this program and have saved a good number of humpbacks themselves.

Humpback caught in a longliner's gill nets

opposite —
Humpbacks lunge feeding for capelin

Humpback Flukes

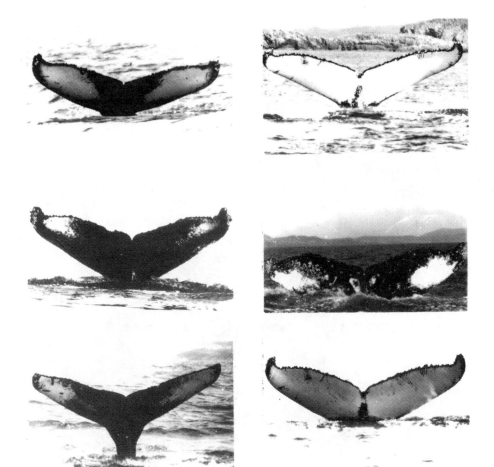

The flukes of each humpback whale have unique patterns which make it possible to recognize individual animals. Although there are some changes which occur in the pattern throughout the animal's life, it is possible to recognize photographs of the same animal taken over a decade and thousands of miles apart. The series of photographs on the left will give you an idea of the variation in individual flukes. In this series one whale has been photographed twice. Try to find the two pictures of the same individual.

The unique fluke patterns are a bit like having all individuals in the population tagged, and this has allowed scientists to carefully track movements of humpbacks. At present, about 1800 individual animals in the northwest Atlantic population have been photographed. These photographs are maintained in a catalogue. With each new photograph the entire catalogue must be searched to check for a match. If a match is made, the researcher can determine where that individual has been before.

From these matches it is known that all humpbacks in the northwest Atlantic winter in the Caribbean. They are therefore a single population.

However, they divide into feeding sub populations. Some humpbacks migrate during summer to the Gulf of Maine. Others come to Newfoundland and Labrador. There are also distinct feeding sub populations that go to Greenland and Iceland. It's interesting that individuals in these sub populations never mix in summer but all return to the same breeding area in winter.

Fluke photographs have enabled scientists to track movements of humpbacks in Newfoundland and Labrador waters as well. It is now known that individual humpbacks travel extensively around the island.

After spending some time in Newfoundland they often go to Labrador. They also, on occasion, move between offshore areas such as the Southeast Shoal and Hamilton Bank, and inshore areas.

Humpbacks spyhopping

A terminal dive sequence of the humpback whale — surfacing to blow — dorsal fin and back appears

Tail stalk comes into view — flukes are raised as the whale dives, leaving his "footprint" on the surface

Fin Whale *(Balaenoptera physalus)*

Common names: Finback, Finner

Identification

- commonly seen offshore and inshore in most areas
- usually in small groups (2-8) — single animals also seen
- very large baleen whale — 60-75 ft. (18-23m) long
- head is wedge-shaped with a distinctive ridge in centre
- right lower jaw and front baleen is white — left lower jaw and baleen is dark
- colour is dark or dark grey on back — belly is light
- behind the head, a pale grey 'V' on the back can sometimes be seen
- flippers are dark on top, light underneath
- flippers comparatively small — about one-ninth of body length
- streamlined body shape — the fin is a sleek, fast swimming whale
- dorsal fin is curved and rather pointed
- fin located about two-thirds of the way back
- minke whales have a similar dorsal fin shape but are a much smaller animal
- dorsals on blue whales appear similar but the fin is smaller and the blue is larger and mottled in colour
- on resurfacing the head appears first — immediately blows
- blow is very tall (15 ft. — 4.5m) and column-shaped
- after blowing, a long back appears — followed after a period by the dorsal fin
- after 5-8 blows a terminal dive is made
- often there is a marked arch to the back
- flukes are almost never exposed in air during a terminal dive

Identification of stranded animals

- most positive trait is the colour difference between the yellowish-white baleen plates on the right jaw and the dark plates on the left
- this can be seen from inside the mouth as well — in case you get swallowed!
- its large size distinguishes it from a minke whale
- 55-100 ventral grooves on the belly that extend beyond navel

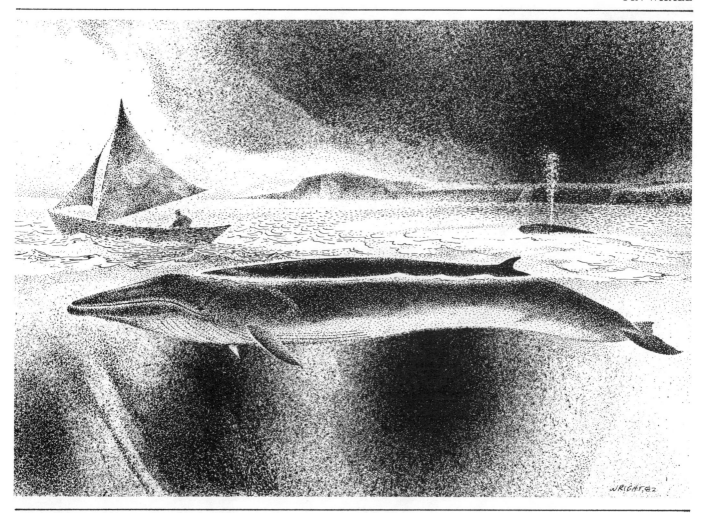

Fin whale surfaces alongside a twenty foot dory

Distribution and Abundance

The fin whale is a common whale throughout the northwest Atlantic of whales in the world. They can be found in all areas where food is plentiful between the ice edge and water masses up to 15 degrees Celsius. There may be as many as 70,000-75,000 fin whales in the world. The population of fin whales in Newfoundland and Labrador waters may be somewhat distinct from fin whales found off Nova Scotia.

In Newfoundland waters in the early years of the 20th century, nearly 500 fin whales were taken per year by whaling stations. Falling catches forced many whaling stations out of business by 1907. In the years from 1945-1951, about 460 fin whales per year were taken by northeast coast whalers. This catch level also produced a noticeably declining population. There were other indications of over-exploitation during this period; smaller-sized animals were captured, lower sighting rates were reported and the whaling industry shifted to other species.

Estimates of the number of fin whales in Newfoundland and Nova Scotia waters range from 6,000-11,000 animals with the best estimate about 8,000. In Newfoundland and Labrador, fin whales can be seen near shore and offshore from early spring until late fall. In winter, they migrate south off the northeast coast, sometimes as far as Florida. In winter, finbacks may also move offshore, although there is minimal evidence of this. Late winter sightings in Newfoundland occur on the south and west coasts. Good places to sight fin whales are off the southeast coast of Newfoundland in early summer, and off southern Labrador in midsummer. Fins are often found inshore in small numbers among large concentrations of humpbacks.

Natural History

Mating by fin whales occurs in warmer waters during winter. Fin whales are sexually mature at about 10 years of age and about 55-60 ft. (16-18m) in length. Females have a calf about every third year. After a gestation period of about 1 year, a 20 ft. (6m) calf weighing 2 tons (1800 kg) is born. The calf nurses for 7 months. At weaning it is about 36 ft. (11m) long. It still has a long of growing to do to reach its 40-50 ton (36-45,000 kg) adult weight. Fin whales may live up to 100 years.

Fin whales are extremely fast swimmers (greater than 20 km/hr). A fin whale radio-tagged in Iceland covered 3,000 km in 10 days!

Although they are commonly seen in groups, little is known of the social organization of fin whales. They are known to produce extremely loud low frequency sounds. The meaning of such sounds is not known but they may function to threaten animals or to communicate with other finbacks over some distance.

Ice entrapments of fin whales have been reported in Newfoundland, most commonly on the west coast. In 1982 a group of about 10 or so were caught in a small lead of water near the Port-au-Port Peninsula. It was several days before the ice receded and the whales were freed. Farley Mowat described the death of a fin whale which was isolated in a shallow cove near Burgeo in his book *A Whale for the Killing*.

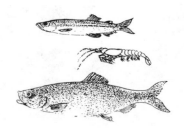

Fin whales feed on krill and small fish. Like all baleen whales, their primary problem is to concentrate prey into compact groups before engulfing it and the water in which it swims. Feeding sequences by fin whales have been observed in which the animal swims toward the prey, rolls on its right side, rapidly pivots in a tight turn and opens its mouth. Such a manoeuvre may allow the whale to take advantage of the white side of its head to scare and concentrate bait and then turn and approach it cryptically.

The colour variations of a fin whale's head
— the left side of head and baleen are dark
— the right side of head and baleen are white
— note also the chevron behind the flippers

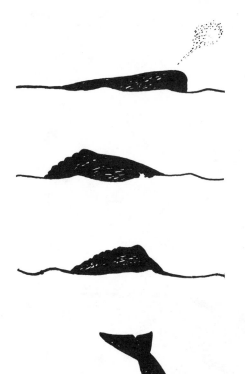

Sperm Whale *(Physeter catadon)*
Common name: Moby Dick

Identification

- largest toothed whale
- common offshore species in deep water - inshore sightings are infrequent
- seen in groups or singly
- sexually dimorphic — males are large, 40-55 ft. (12-17m)
- females from 25-38 ft. (7.5 - 12m)
- head is square and appears above water when the animal blows
- blowhole is well forward on head and located to left of midline
- coloration is dark brown/grey — body has a wrinkled appearance
- males commonly have many scars on body
- flippers are short and robust
- dorsal hump appears as a low fat fin
- many females have a distinct callus on the forward portion of hump — this is lacking in males
- series of lumps or knuckles behind the dorsal hump
- tail flukes are large and powerful - all dark
- when surfacing the blunt head appears above water
- blow is directed forward and to the left
- blows tend to be very noisy
- head and blow are sighted first, then the back is visible
- usually the animal lies at the surface, quite stationary
- blows for 10 minutes or so — often blows 20-50 times before diving
- when diving the head disappears
- back is arched so that the dorsal lump and knuckles are exposed
- dives are usually nearly vertical
- flukes are lifted into the air
- dives are deep and may last a long time (from 30-60 minutes)

Identification of stranded animals

- most positive traits are blunt, square head
- narrow white lower jaw with 18-25 large teeth

WRIGHT '82

Distribution and Abundance

Sperm whales are found in all oceans of the world. The greatest concentrations are in areas near deep water and where currents converge. Although exact figures are not available, it is believed that there are several hundred thousand sperm whales worldwide. A somewhat larger population exists in the Southern Hemisphere than in the Northern.

In the northwest Atlantic, they range from the Davis Strait all the way to South America. Distribution and movement varies between males and females, although there is a general northward migration in summer, and a return to southern portions of the range in winter. Males tend to travel further north while groups of females and immature males are found between 30-50 degrees latitude. Sightings are typically made in offshore locations.

Battle with a giant squid

The sperm whale blow — the single nostril is set well forward and to the left

Natural History

Sperm whales were made famous by Melville's *Moby Dick*, and were the mainstay of North American whaling. While common in Newfoundland and Labrador waters as a deep water species, they are not typically seen from shore. Strandings of single animals have been reported in a variety of inshore locations. Catches of sperm whales in Newfoundland waters during whaling days were very low.

Sperm whales, the largest of the toothed whales, eat squid, preferably large squid. The heads of these whales are usually scarred by sucker rings from battles with giant squid. Sometimes they even swallow the squid whole. The squid may struggle inside the whale too, as sucker marks have been found on the stomach walls of sperm whales. Very few of these battles have been reliably documented, which is understandable as they probably occur at great depths.

Sucker imprints of giant squid on the skin of the sperm whale have been found which were about 3 inches in diameter. This means the squid could have been well over 70 ft. (21m) long if length increases proportionally with sucker size.

When a sperm whale is dying it often vomits the contents of its stomach. A few giant squid were discovered at whaling stations because of this reaction. Squid beaks are often found in the intestines of sperm whales. A waxy substance is secreted by the whale's stomach around the beaks. This is ambergris, a rare substance that was once highly prized for use in making perfumes.

An adult male may eat up to one ton of squid per day. Because of the difference in distribution between males and females, and the very large head of the male (which may be an adaptation to deep diving), it is thought that males and females may exploit somewhat different food.

Sperm whales are capable of extremely deep dives. Dives over 3,000 ft. (900m) have been recorded. Several animals have become entangled in submarine cables during deep dives.

Sperm whales reach puberty at about 10 years of age; although males may mature much later. Males are in excess of 40 ft. (12 m) and females about 30 ft. (9 m) at maturity. Mature females join a harem group of other females with a male harem master. Every few years each female produces a 13 ft. (4 m) calf after a gestation period of 14-16 months. Lactation lasts for at least one year and sometimes up to two years.

After weaning her calf, the female rests for nearly a year before breeding again. Thus the breeding cycle is 3-4 years. Weight of the adults averages about 40 tons (36,000 kg) for males and 22 tons (20,000 kg) for females.

Sperm whales are very social and form a variety of groups including harem schools, nursery schools, juvenile schools, bachelor schools and bull schools. Lone bulls are also found, especially in colder waters.

While most females reproduce, it is believed that competition between males to serve as harem masters limits the number of males that actually reproduce to a percentage of those available. The gregarious nature of sperm whales is also seen in their tendency to mass strand which has been reported in various parts of the world.

Vocalizations by sperm whales consist of clicks. Some clicks are used as echolocation signals to find prey and objects. Another click is produced in a pattern much like a telegraph message. These vocalizations are called codas. These codas may be used to identify individuals and to signal their position.

The long ardous whaling trips gave rise to the whaler's handicraft called scrimshaw. Artists would polish and engrave sperm whale teeth with beautiful designs and scenes depicting whaling. The teeth of sperm whales are particularly suited to scrimshaw because of their large size. When teeth from stranded sperm whales and other species are available local artists such as Jim Troke of Twillingate, can beautifully recreate this unique art form.

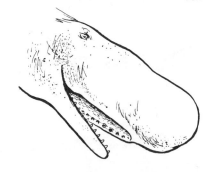

The sperm whale's teeth are found only on the narrow lower jaw and fit into sockets in the upper jaw

Sei Whale *(Balaenoptera borealis)*

pronounced 'say'

Identification

- commonly seen in small numbers in summer off Newfoundland
- offshore stock is present year round in the Labrador Sea
- often seen singly, or in groups of 2-10
- length under 50 ft. (15m) — average about 44 ft. (13.5m); streamlined body
- not as slender as a fin whale — not as robust as a minke
- head is flat and wedge-shaped with central ridge
- line of mouth arched; coloration on both sides of head is dark
- can be distinguished from fin whales by approaching on right side of whale - fins have white on right lower jaw, sei do not
- baleen plates are dark-black with white bristles
- coloration of back is dark grey — sides are dark — underside is lighter grey
- there may be lighter spots on the back and sides
- flippers are all dark — relatively small
- dorsal fin is fairly large, located less than two-thirds of the way back
- shape of dorsal fin is similar to fin whale but typically more hooked — dorsal fin is located farther forward than dorsal of fin or blue
- flukes are all dark
- when surfacing to blow, head may be seen
- often head, back and dorsal fin all appear at about same time, just after the blow
- blow is cone shaped - like fin or blue blow but not as high
- may blow several times and then dive for short period
- 5-6 blows may occur followed by longer dive
- in terminal dive there is generally less arching of the back than a fin
- in terminal dive sei whales appear to sink; flukes do not show above water

Identification of stranded animals

- ventral grooves (38-56) end well before navel
- dark baleen plates on both sides with fine white bristles
- if the animal is fresh, body coloration will help

WRIGHT '82

Distribution and Abundance

In general, distribution, migrations and abundance of the sei whale are not well known. They are distributed in all oceans, usually in warmer water. Typically sightings occur in deep waters, usually over 330 ft. (100m), and they are infrequently seen in coastal waters. There may be a seasonal north-south migration. World-wide numbers as high as 80,000 individuals have been suggested.

From tagging, there is some evidence of two discrete stocks in the northwest Atlantic, with one centre of abundance in Nova Scotia and another in the Labrador Sea. From 1966 to 1972 over 800 whales were landed by whalers in eastern Canadian water but in general the catch of sei whales was never heavy. Sei whales in the northwest Atlantic may number around 2,000 animals; the Labrador Sea stock probably numbers about 1,000.

Natural History

Sei whales are skimmer feeders as well as gulpers, and eat almost any kind of plankton and some small fish. Feeding probably takes place year round and the animals congregate in areas of plankton blooms. During skim-feeding, the animal swims slowly through the water with its mouth open. By actively feeding it is able to satisfy its need for approximately 1 ton (900 kg) of food per day.

Sei whales reach maturity at about 10 years of age when males are about 40 ft. (12m) long and females are about 43 ft. (13m). There is some evidence that sei whales form pair bonds which may last for some period of time. Breeding is most common in the fall. After a 12 month gestation a one ton (900 kg) calf is born. Lactation lasts about 6 months. The reproductive cycle for females appears to be two years long. Longevity is probably about 70 years.

opposite — A comparison of three species commonly confused

Blue whale — head U-shaped, dorsal fin small and well back

Fin whale — white on right side of the head, slender, dorsal larger than blue whale and two thirds back

Sei whale — relatively large dorsal fin further forward

Blue whale

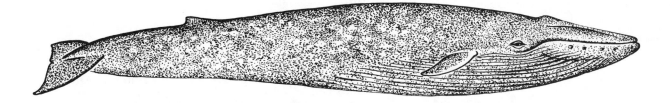

Fin whale

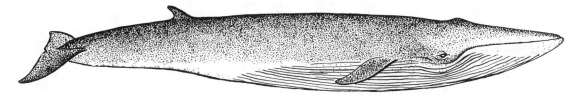

Sei whale

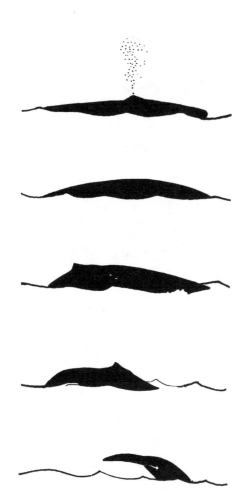

Blue Whale *(Balaenoptera musculus)*

Common name: Sulphur-bottom, the Biggest Kind

Identification

- uncommon but regular sightings in some areas
- seen singly, in pairs, or small groups
- the largest baleen whale — the largest animal that has ever lived
- males from 70-85 ft. (21-26m) — females from 75-90 ft. (23-28m)
- very broad 'U'-shaped head — all dark grey with central ridge
- long streamlined body
- coloration is pale blue-grey to dark and black
- coloration is mottled with irregular spots
- flippers are short — about one-tenth of body length
- flippers are dark on top, light underneath
- dorsal fin is far back and very small
- often, fin only visible just before animal is about to dive
- flukes are large and all dark
- when resurfacing, blow is a slender vertical column up to 30 ft. (9 m) tall
- head and blow hole may remain visible when small dorsal fin appears if the animal is moving slowly
- if the animal is moving more rapidly, the dorsal fin is only seen on about one blow in five
- flukes sometimes raised just above water in a terminal dive
- flukes at a 60 degree angle, not straight up in the air

Identification of stranded animals

- the most positive trait — its large size
- dark baleen plates on both sides
- broad 'U' shaped head
- dark, mottled coloration may be intact on fresh specimens
- there are from 55-58 ventral grooves that extend to the navel

opposite — the trap skiff with dory in tow is not as long as the blue whale

Distribution and Abundance

Blue whales are found worldwide, but because of their large size and food requirements, they are most common in productive polar waters. Because of intense whaling pressure, the animal is now protected and considered rare in most locations.

Blue whale sightings in Newfoundland and Labrador waters are infrequent. There have been recent sightings in Placentia and Trinity Bays, as well as on the west coast and in several offshore locations.

Early Newfoundland whaling killed up to 275 animals per year during their migration to or from Davis Strait. Present numbers in Newfoundland and Labrador waters are believed to be in the low hundreds.

During the summer there is a small population that is reliably sighted around the Mingan Islands in the Gulf of St. Lawrence. In late winter and early spring, blue whales appear along the ice edge on Newfoundland's west coast and along the south coast between Port-aux-Basques and Fortune Bay. In 1982, four blue whales stranded and died along the west coast when ice forced them to shore. Blue whales in other ice strandings have occasionally been towed to safety by Canadian Coast Guard icebreakers. It is believed that as the ice recedes, the animals return to the Gulf.

Natural History

Born after a gestation period of 11-12 months, a baby blue is 23-27 ft. (7-8m) long and weighs about 3 tons (2700 kg). As a calf it grows at a rate of about 9 lbs. (4 kg) an hour, or 200 lbs. (90 kg) per day!

At 7 months, when it is weaned, it is 50 ft. (15m) or so long and weighs 20 tons (18,000 kg). Females are typically larger than males. Both males and females mature at about 75 ft. (23m). The blue whale is the largest animal that has ever lived; larger even than the biggest dinosaur. A female blue whale of 106 ft. (32.5m) and 150 tons (135,000 kg) has been recorded.

drawings to scale

46

Recently it was found that blue whales may be individually identified or recognized from photographs of the mottled pigmentation around the dorsal fin. A catalogue of these photographs was recently begun. If such a program is successful, it will allow scientists to accurately learn about movements and social groups as well as to census blue whales.

Mottled pigmentation visible as the whale surfaces

Blue whales feed primarily on krill or red bait. Inshore sightings of this whale in Newfoundland tend to occur during April-May, when breeding swarms of krill are found. They consume 2-4 tons (18-36,000 kg) per day; a 3,000,000 calorie/day diet.

The social life of blue whales is poorly detailed. Blues are often seen in groups, although groupings may change over a period of hours. There is little known of the communication system of blue whales as well.

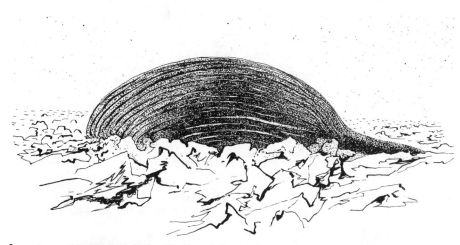

Krill — shown life-size, the staple food of the largest living animal

Ice-entrapped dead blue whale with distended ventral grooves

Right Whale *(Eubalaena glacialis)*

Identification

- very rare in Newfoundland and Labrador waters
- occasional reports of sightings in Trinity Bay and Bonavista Bay
- may occur elsewhere
- recent sightings in our waters have been of individuals
- in other areas small groups are common
- large baleen whale about 50 ft. (15m) long
- large head (25 percent of body length)
- series of lumps or callosities on head, in front of blowhole
- callosities are light coloured — may protrude as far as 4 in. (10 cm)
- two blow holes are widely separated
- if feeding, the head and long baleen plates (up to 7 ft./2m) may be visible at the surface
- baleen is light in front, dark in back
- the body is round and stocky with a broad fat back
- no ventral grooves and the dorsal fin is absent
- color is black but there may be light scars
- may be white patches under the chin and around the navel
- calves are often much lighter than adults
- because of the wide separation of the blowholes, when the whale resurfaces two distinct low, bushy spouts appear in a 'V' shape
- after blowing at the surface for 5-10 minutes, the animal dives
- when diving, the tail flukes are thrown high in the air
- flukes have pointed tips, a deep notch and are dark below

Identification of stranded animals

- most positive traits are absence of a dorsal fin and throat grooves
- mouth shape and long dark baleen plates
- callosities on the head are also obvious traits

WRIGHT '82

Distribution and Abundance

Whaling activities reduced right whales to critically low numbers and its original range is not well known. In the northwest Atlantic it is believed to have been abundant from the Davis Straits as far south as Florida. Small groups of animals are known off Iceland, in the Bay of Fundy and off Nova Scotia and Cape Cod. These areas may have been traditional mating and calving regions, but now contain only remnant populations.

Migration movements are poorly known. Right whales probably engage in annual migrations between high latitude summer feeding grounds and lower latitude wintering grounds. There have been only a couple of sightings of right whales in Newfoundland in the past decade. You'll be lucky if you see one.

Natural History

The name right whale indicates that it was the 'right' whale to kill during whaling. They were fairly slow, could be predictably found in coastal waters, and did not sink when harpooned, so they were a favourite target. Overhunting has decimated its numbers in the northwest Atlantic. Whaling voyages from the 1700s on rarely caught a right whale. The International Whaling Commission has protected right whales since 1937.

Mature length for either sex is about 50 ft. (15m), although 60 ft. (18m) animals are known. After a gestation of 9-10 months a single calf of about 18 ft. (5.5m) is born usually during winter in a protected, shallow bay. After weaning at about 1 year the calf may remain in contact with the mother for another 2-3 years. There are descriptions of play between mothers and calves lasting hours at a time.

The right whale is a relative of the bowhead whale which has adapted to year round living in the Arctic. The bowhead can be distinguished from the right whale by its white pigmentation on the chin and lower jaw.

Right Whale Feeding

Both bowheads and right whales feed by skimming small plankton from the water. During feeding, the animal swims through the water near the surface with its mouth open. Water and plankton enter the mouth then water passes out through the baleen plates leaving the plankton on the inside of the plates. In Newfoundland waters, the basking shark filter feeds on plankton in a similar manner, swimming along with its mouth open and filtering the bait through gill rakers.

Filter feeding —
above — right whale
below — basking shark

Medium-sized Whales

Whales drawn to scale based on a 20 ft. dory. Whales are ranked on how commonly they are observed. Whales at the top of this page are more commonly seen than whales at the bottom of the page.

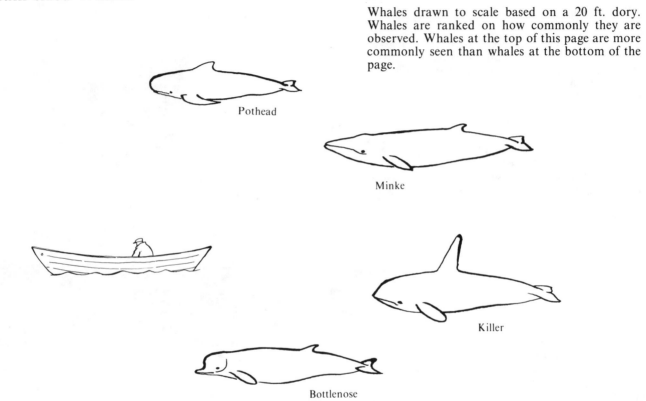

Pothead

Minke

Killer

Bottlenose

Key information in identifying medium-sized whales

	Fin Shape	Coloration	Group Size
Pothead		All dark	Large
Minke		All dark	Single or several animals
Bottlenose		All dark	4-10 animals
Killer		White patch visible	4-10 animals

Pothead Whale *(Globicephala melaena)*

Common names: Pilot Whale, Blackfish

Identification

- commonly seen inshore in summer where squid are abundant
- always seen in groups from 5-200 animals
- groups of 20-50 animals are most common inshore
- groups consist of animals of both sexes and of various sizes
- during summer this includes newborn calves 5-6 ft. (1.5-1.8 m)
- large males may reach 20 ft. (6 m)
- females are smaller — 14-18 ft. (4.5-5.5m)
- head is visible when animal blows
- head is thick and bulbous — shaped like a pot
- toothed whale — 20-22 teeth in upper jaws
- coloration is black except for light grey anchor-shaped pattern under the head and a light band extending along the belly
- newly-born young are noticeably lighter in colour and mottled
- usually individuals surface to blow at different times
- flippers are long and distinctly pointed
- the dorsal fin is heavy with a long base — low in profile
- the blow can be seen close up but is inconspicuous at a distance
- in resurfacing usually the 'pothead' can be seen
- blowing in a group is irregular
- it is difficult to follow the blowing pattern of any one animal
- a group may spend a period blowing, and then change behaviour for a while with little time spent at the surface
- on occasion, spy-hopping, lob-tailing and breaching can be seen
- young animals sometimes swim on their back or sides at the surface, rapidly flapping their flippers in the air

Identification of stranded animals

- in Newfoundland waters, potheads mass strand fairly commonly and several individuals may be found on a beach in the same area

opposite - Fishermen haul trawls amidst a group of pothead whales

Distribution and Abundance

Potheads are one of the most common inshore species, especially during a good squid year. When squid (Illex illecebrosus), the whales primary food, are abundant, many potheads can be seen. Sometimes this is as early as May, but more typically they are first seen in July and as late as October. To find potheads, check with local fishermen and ask them if the squid are in the area.

Earlier estimates of pothead abundance in Newfoundland waters were as high as 50,000 individuals. Whaling for this species in Newfoundland was done by driving groups of animals ashore, primarily in Trinity and Bonavista Bays. One year, in the mid-1950s, about 10,000 animals were killed in Newfoundland. Whaling was discontinued in 1972 because of substantially decimated local stocks and poor markets for the meat in fur farms. Present numbers are not accurately known but it is a common and abundant whale.

In winter, potheads are presumed to range from the Grand Banks as far south as North Carolina.

Natural History

Female pothead whales mature at 6 years and about 12 ft. (3.5m) in length. Males mature at 12 years and about 16 Males mature at 12 years and about 16 ft. (5m) in length. Mature adult males can weigh as much as three tons (2,700 kg), although two tons (1,800 kg) is more common. Adult females may weigh two tons (1,800 kg). At birth calves weigh slightly over 200 lbs. (190 kg). They are born after a pregnancy of 16 months. Calves then suckle for about 20 months until they are weaned.

The social cohesiveness of groups of pothead whales is well known. Even when driven ashore by whalers, the groups would not disband. It is rare to see a single individual. The groups seen inshore around Newfoundland typically contain animals of both sexes with a wide range of ages. The males may compete for breeding privileges so that a hierarchy excludes smaller males. It is also possible that larger groups are composed of smaller, close-knit groups which are stable over some period of time. There is some evidence that females in a group may help nurse each other's young.

Potheads are one of the noisiest whales in Newfoundland. Their group structure requires social communication, and they orient to prey and objects by echolocation. Vocalizations include a wide variety of whistles and clicks.

The best place to look for potheads is where fishermen are catching squid. One of the best squid areas is Holyrood Arm in Conception Bay. While feeding, a group of potheads may circle the bait but other formations are also seen.

Spy hopping — note anchor pattern

Occasionally, groups of potheads are found stranded on shore. Mass strandings are a natural phenomenon and have been observed throughout history. Their frequency seems related to the relative abundance of potheads in inshore waters. In a mass stranding, all animals in a group slowly swim ashore. The reason for such strandings is not understood. Explanations are generally of two kinds. One is that there is something wrong with the animals or at least with key members of the group. This could be sickness, or parasites that affect their navigation abilities. The second explanation is that there is something unusual about the stranding site. Strandings usually occur at gently sloping, sandy beaches, which may distort the whale's sonar echoes, just as they can a boat's sonar. Some scientists have suggested that mass strandings occur at sites where there are unusual magnetic fields. The presence of bait very close to shore may also be a factor. It is probably best to think of mass strandings like any accident where, rather than a single cause, a number of factors probably contribute. See the section on strandings for more information.

A minke whale swims by a fisherman hauling his salmon net

Minke Whale *(Balaenoptera acutorostrata)*

Common names: Mink Whales, Herring Hog, sometimes Grampus

Identification

- a common whale in all waters around Newfoundland and Labrador
- the smallest baleen whale
- maximum length is 30 ft. (9m) — more commonly 24-26 ft. (7-8m)
- usually seen close to shore and singly
- may be seen offshore and in small groups
- a narrow, triangular shaped head, with a central ridge
- head is black — shading to white under lower jaw
- baleen is white
- flippers are about 10 percent of body length
- conspicious band of white on each flipper
- back is black with occasionally visible broad light band from behind the flippers up the side
- dorsal fin is tall, extremely pointed and hooked slightly backward - located in last one-third of the back
- underside is light grey/white
- about 60 throat grooves which end well before navel, just after the flippers
- flukes are dark on top - light on the bottom
- when resurfacing the pointed head often can be seen followed quickly by blow
- blow is low and inconspicuous
- commonly blows several times and then submerges
- on resurfacing often moving in a different direction
- blow and dorsal fin visible at the same time
- usually 2-6 blows, and then a dive for 2-4 minutes
- in a terminal dive the back is sharply arched
- flukes do not come above water
- may sometimes be seen lunge-feeding, but more often dive for fish

Identification of stranded animals

- most positive trait is the band of white on flippers
- yellowish white baleen plates (300-325 per side — maximum length 4 in. (12 cm)
- 50-70 ventral grooves that extend only to navel

Distribution and Abundance

Minke whales are the most common baleen whales and occur worldwide. World population is estimated at about 200,000. There are no reliable estimates for the northwest Atlantic. Estimates of the numbers of this whale may be biased by their tendency to approach boats.

They are first seen in inshore Newfoundland and Labrador waters in April; a few as early as March. They are sighted throughout the summer and fall as late as October-November, although some animals remain into the winter. Ice entrapments in winter have been reported. Minke whales summer north from Cape Cod and winter as far south as Florida.

above — There are over 300 yellowish-white baleen plates on each side of a minke's upper jaw.
below — Detail of baleen plates

Minke Whale Feeding

This whale has a rather varied diet eating planktonic crustaceans as well as herring, capelin, and mackerel. Squid may also be a part of their diet.

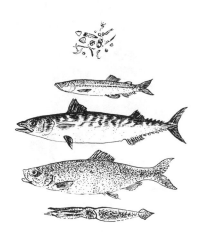

Minke whales feeding on capelin engulf great quantities of fish and water by expanding the ventral throat grooves. The water is forced out by the tongue, and the baleen plates retain the fish.

Natural History

Minkes reach sexual maturity at about 7 years of age and a length of 23-25 ft. (7m). Mature weights average from 6-8 tons (54,000-72,000 kg). After a gestation period of 10-11 months, a 1,000 lb. (450 kg) calf is born, and suckles for 6 months. This allows females to reproduce as frequently as every 18 months, faster than all other baleen whales. Longevity of minke whales is believed to be about 50 years.

Minke whales are currently the species most subject to whaling. Since 1972, there has been no whaling in Canadian waters and the numbers of this species are not known to be depleted. In the 1960s, whaling for minkes centred in Dildo, Trinity Bay. The flesh was marketed locally as 'arctic steak'.

Studies of the social organization of minke whales are just beginning. Some individual minkes can be identified by photographs. In some areas, minkes maintain exclusive ranges for a substantial part of the summer season, which is believed to be unique among baleen whales. Vocalizations have been recorded, and are generally low frequency grunts or higher frequency pulsed sounds.

Minkes have the reputation of being 'curious' about boats and fishing gear. That may be true, but minkes may also be using man as a guide and help in fishing. In the summer of 1978, Norm Keilly of St. Mary's watched as a minke whale repeatedly made trips to a herring net he had just cleaned. After a dozen or so round trips in a half hour, the net sank. Norm feared that the whale had hit and damaged the net, so he hauled it in. To his astonishment, he picked 4,800 pounds (2,000 kg) of herring from the net! The whale must have been driving fish towards the net and using it as a trap to help it catch fish.

opposite — The white banded flipper of the minke is often visible through the water

WRIGHT '82

Killer Whale (Orcinus orca)

Common names: Orca, Blackfish

Identification

- sightings are infrequent but small numbers are usually seen
  during summer months throughout Newfoundland and Labrador waters
- from ice entrapments, they are known to occur around here in winter as well
- usually seen in small groups of from 3-10 animals
- robust body with a round blunt head
- length of males up to 32 ft. (10m), females to 27 ft. (7m)
- head is black with oval white patch just above and behind eye
- underside of head is white
- flippers are large and round — black
- very large, triangular dorsal fin
- dorsal fins of females and immature animals less than 3 ft.tall (1m)
- dorsal on males enormous — up to 6 ft. (1.8m) tall
- black back in front of dorsal fin
- behind dorsal fin is greyish saddle visible in photographs or at close quarters
- there is enough variation in eye patch, saddle and dorsal fin to make some
  individuals recognizable at a distance
- white pattern from underside of head continues on the belly
  then divides and extends up the sides of the animal
- most conspicuous field traits are large dorsal fin of males and patches of white
- the group tends to resurface together for a series of 4-6 short shallow dives
- blows are visible as well as head and eye patch
- may move fast — speeds up to 50 kph have been recorded
- spy-hopping, breaching or lob-tailing are seen on occasion

Identification of stranded animals

- most positive traits are the white patches
- 10-12 large teeth on each side of both jaws
- large dorsal fins

opposite — A fisherman watches as killer whales surface and dive by his anchored dory

Distribution and Abundance

Orcas are found in all oceans but are never abundant. Sightings in the Northwest Atlantic have been reported from the pack ice south to the Caribbean. They seem to prefer coastal areas and can sometimes be seen in bays. Movements in the northwest Atlantic are poorly known but probably correspond with that of their prey. Sightings in Newfoundland and Labrador waters are most common in summer; more northerly sightings occur later in summer. Orcas have been sighted most frequently in Trinity, Bonavista and St. Mary's Bays, the Strait of Belle Isle, and just off St. John's. Ice entrapments and sightings confirm their occurrence in our waters year round. There are no reliable estimates of numbers in Newfoundland and Labrador waters.

Natural History

Killer whales have been intensively studied off the west coast of British Columbia and Washington, but there has been little work in Newfoundland and Labrador waters. Because of captivity in ocean zoos where they are extremely trainable, orcas are a popular whale and the topic of many legends.

By photographing the dorsal fin and the patterns on the back directly around it, orcas can be individually identified. On the west coast of Canada, a catalogue of such photos has allowed scientists to follow groups of orcas for years. A catalogue of orca photographs has only recently been started for Newfoundland and Labrador waters.

Killer whales may live for up to 35 years. At the end of a 12 month pregnancy, a 9 ft. (3m) calf of 400 lbs (180 kg) is born and then nursed for one year. Males reach maturity at a length of 20 ft. (6m) and females at 16 ft. (5m). Average mature length is 27 ft. (8m) with a maximum of 32 ft. (10m) and a weight of 8 tons (7,200 kg) for males. Maximum female size is 28 ft. (8.5m)

Individual differences between dorsal fin and back patterns

Killer Whale Feeding

The basic social unit appears to be an extended family with about 20 percent males; 20 percent calves and the remainder made up of females and immature animals. Such groups remain together for life and travel as a close cohesive unit. There is evidence of cooperative hunting. Vocalization consists of a variety of whistles and there is evidence that different groups are recognizable by unique dialects. Echolocation sounds are relatively low frequency clicks which probably reflect their need to find larger prey than most whales.

Killer whales feed on fish, squid, seabirds and other marine mammals. Each day they eat about 4 percent of their body weight. Small prey is swallowed whole; larger prey is torn apart and then swallowed. There are records of pods of killer whales attacking and eating large whales. Researchers from Memorial University have observed killer whales attacking adult humpback whales on the Southeast Shoal on several occasions. Large (bite-size) pieces of humpback blubber could be seen floating on the water after the attacks. From their observations the scientists could not tell if the killer whales were actually trying to kill and eat the humpbacks or just drive them out of the area.

There is little evidence that orcas pose a threat to man and documented cases of attack are rare. Like all large wild animals, however, orcas should be treated with respect and caution.

A spy-hopping killer whale

Northern Bottlenose Whale *(Hyperoodon ampullatus)*

Identification

- common in deep water (around 3000 ft./1000m) off Labrador
- in summer there are some sightings in inshore Labrador waters
- unusual in water shallower than 600 ft. (180m)
- a medium-sized whale — average length is about 30 ft. (9m)
- seen in groups, often densely packed
- solitary animals, probably males, are also seen
- blunt forehead and beak
- bulbous forehead is most pronounced in males and large females
- there is a noticeable neck line — robust body
- flippers relatively small and dark
- dorsal fin is sickle-shaped — located about two-thirds back
- there is no notch in the flukes
- coloration is variable — calves are dark-brownish in colour
- patchy areas of lighter colours develop with age
- extremely large animals may have light-coloured heads
- in general, appear a light chocolate brown
- flippers, flukes, and dorsal all remain dark
- often resurfaces sharply so that the head and beak are visible
- a low, bushy blow (3-6 ft./1-2m)
- whale usually stays at the surface between blows
- head, back and dorsal exposed at the same time
- after several minutes (as long as 10) at surface, animal dives for a long period,
- frequently as long as 30 minutes
- in a terminal dive, flukes are thrown high in air

Identification of stranded animals

- most positive traits are unnotched tail fluke
- only two teeth in lower jaw
- two throat grooves forming a 'V' shape on the chin
- the bulbous head and beak are distinct
- mass strandings have been recorded

Distribution and Abundance

Northern bottlenose whales are restricted to Arctic and north temperate waters, primarily in offshore areas from Davis Strait as far south as Rhode Island. Most sightings in our waters are confined to areas adjacent to Labrador in early summer, often near the ice edge. Stocks are believed to be critically depleted because of past whaling.

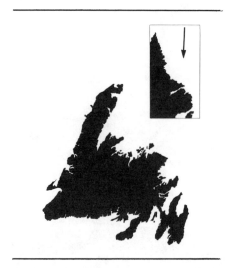

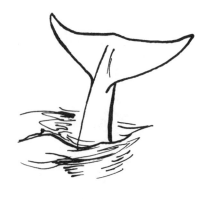

A lob-tailing bottlenose whale

Natural History

The northern bottlenose averages about 30 ft. (9m) for males with a maximum of 33 ft. (10m) and a weight of 4 tons (3,600 kg). Females are somewhat smaller, 24 ft. (7.5m) long and weigh 3.5 tons (3,200 kg). Males and females become sexually mature between 8-12 years. After a 12 month gestation period, a 10 ft. (3m) calf is born. There is some evidence that lactation lasts up to 1 year. It is likely that most females have a 2 year reproductive cycle. The lifespan of the bottlenose whale is at least 37 years.

Apart from the observation that most bottlenose whales are seen in pairs or groups, or occasionally as solitary males, little is known of their social organization. There are numerous observations of groups of bottlenose whales aiding an injured companion. Bottlenose whales are fascinated by ships and attracted to unusual sounds. In 1980, small groups of bottlenose whales often approached the Ben Ocean Lancer, a drilling rig, off Labrador. For long periods of time the animals would stay with the rig. Of greatest interest were the huge thrusters, which would attract and excite the animals. When excited, they often lob-tail.

Food for the bottlenose whale is primarily squid but they are also known to take herring and some starfish. They are one of the deepest and longest divers of all cetacea. Dives may last from 14 to 70 minutes, to depths as much as 3,000 ft. (900m).

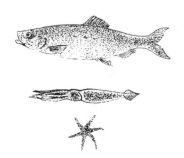

Small Whales

Whales drawn to scale based on a 20 ft. dory. Whales are ranked on how commonly they are observed. Whales at the top of this page are more commonly seen than whales at the bottom of the page.

Harbour Porpoise

White-Sided Dolphin

White-Beaked Dolphin

Common Dolphin

Beluga

Narwhal

Key information in identifying small whales

	Group Size	Dorsal Fin	Coloration
Harbour porpoise	Single animal, pairs or small group	Present	Black back
White-sided dolphin	Larger group	Present	Black back
White-beaked dolphin	Larger group	Present	Patches of white or grey in front and back of dorsal
Beluga	Single animal, pairs or small group	None	White
Narwhal	Single animal, pairs or small group	None	Mottled

Harbour porpoise *(Phocoena phocoena)*
Common names: Puffin Pig, Puffins, Common Porpoise

Identification

- the smallest cetacean — 4-6 ft. (1.2-1.8m) in length
- perhaps most commonly seen cetacean in Newfoundland and Labrador
- waters
- seen inshore in small groups, in pairs or single animals
- females with young are also seen
- groups do not appear to move in formation
- only brief glimpses of the animal are possible
- very small chunky body
- usually shy and difficult to approach
- coloration is dark grey or black on back
- light grey patches on sides — white under chin and on belly
- small flippers on the sides all dark
- flippers located completely in white portion of side coloration
- dorsal fin is broad and fairly heavy
- fin roughly triangular with a concave trailing edge
- fin appears large when scaled to portion of visible back
- flukes are dark on both sides
- usually resurfaces for series of blows each 15-20 seconds — then dives for 3-6
- minutes
- blows are commonly heard in calm weather but not seen

Identification of stranded animals

- most positive traits are small robust body
- small teeth (22-28 per jaw)

Distribution and Abundance

Harbour porpoises are common in the cooler waters of the north Atlantic and Pacific. In the northwest Atlantic they have been seen from Davis Strait to North Carolina. Although it is the most commonly seen cetacean, little is known of its movements and numbers. They are most commonly seen in summer months, but ice entrapments in winter have also occurred. There may be an offshore and southerly movement in winter. Frequently these porpoises are accidently caught in inshore fishing gear in Newfoundland and Labrador waters.

Natural History

Although small, harbour porpoises are heavy (90-200 lbs/40-90 kg). Females are mature and able to breed as early as 14 months, more typically at 3-4 years. Males reach maturity in their third year, when about 4 ft./1.2m) long. After a gestation of 10-11 months, an 11 lb. (5 kg) calf is born. The calf suckles and stays with the mother for about 8 months. Females usually become pregnant again the following year.

Harbour porpoises feed on schooling and bottom fish including mackerel, herring and cod. They eat approximately 9-11 lbs. (4-5) kg) of food per day. Choice of prey probably depends on local abundance.

Although difficult to see in the water, harbour porpoise can sometimes be seen up close, on a wharf, when they become entangled in gill nets

White-sided Dolphin *(Lagenorhynchus acutus)*
Common names: Jumper, Squidhound

Identification

- very active, fast-moving dolphin
- usually seen in groups of 20-50 animals
- larger groups are occasionally seen offshore
- seen inshore during summer — offshore during other times of year
- other times of the year seen offshore
- may be seen associated with potheads or white-beaked dolphins
- feeding on squid
- fast swimming and acrobatic — often seen in low breaches
- small beak, but well pronounced — always dark
- lower jaw and chin white up to eye — grey above eye
- back is black
- yellow stripe on side beginning at dorsal
- darker yellow on top, lighter on bottom
- brighter yellow can often be seen when animal surfaces to blow
- flippers are all black - roughly triangular and pointed
- dorsal is large, hooked backward and pointed
- below yellow on side is band of grey — belly is white
- flukes are dark
- resurfaces as a group swimming quickly
- blows several times per minute
- may be confused with white-beaked dolphin — look for colour on side
- of white-sided dolphins

Identification of stranded animals

- yellowish colour on sides darkens in death
- coloration is best identification characteristic to avoid confusion with
- white-beaks
- known to mass strand

opposite — A group of playful white-sided dolphins leap and bowride around a dory-skiff

Distribution and Abundance

Primarily found in waters between the Gulf Stream and the Labrador Current, although they can be seen throughout Newfoundland waters. They are usually seen around the southern parts of the island, and are often found with pothead whales. Their northwest Atlantic distribution is from the Davis Strait to New York. There are no reliable estimates on their numbers. Occasionally, white-sides are accidentally caught in fishing gear.

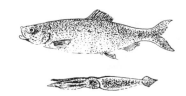

Natural History

The common name for white-sided dolphins in Newfoundland and Labrador is "jumper," appropriate because of the tendency of this speedy dolphin to breach. The names "squidhound" and "jumper" seem to be interchangeable with "white-sides" and "whitebeaks" in different parts of the province.

The social organization of the groups is not known, but they are composed of both males and females. They seem to be different types of groups; some contain only young animals, others· are composed of mature males, females and offspring.

Mature animals of both sexes average about 8 ft. (2.4m) long to a maximum of 10 ft. (3m). Weight ranges from 420 lbs. (190 kg) to 550 lbs. (250 kg.). Calves are born after a gestation of 10 months, usually in April or May. Calves weigh 75 lbs. (35 kg) at birth and suckle for up to 18 months. Age of maturity is about 4-6 years for males (7 ft./2m in length), and 5-8 years for females (7 ft./2m in length).

White-sided dolphins eat mainly fish, including herring and squid.

Comparison of colour patterns
above — white-sided dolphin
centre — white-beaked dolphin
below — white-beaked variation

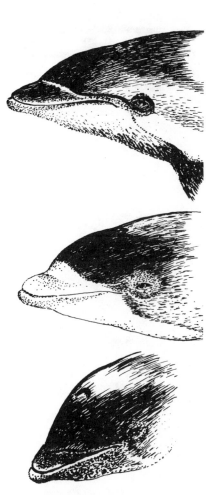

White-beaked Dolphin *(Lagenorhychus albirostris)*

Common names: Squidhound, Jumper

Identification

- common dolphin in Newfoundland and especially Labrador waters
- seen inshore in summer
- from ice entrapments known to occur here in winter also
- seen in small groups of 5-25 animals
- larger groups of over 100 also reported
- mature animals 9-10 ft. (2.7-3.0 m)
- some groups of slightly smaller animals
- the beak is short but distinct — often is white or pale grey
- flippers, dorsal fin and flukes are dark
- lighter grey areas appear on the sides just before dorsal fin and on back just after dorsal
- dorsal fin is triangular in shape with rounded tip
- underside from end of mouth to flukes is light grey
- seen in groups that do not leap from the water
- while moving rapidly, surfacing members of a group breach irregularly over several minutes
- look carefully at the head and beak — some white-beaked dolphins have
- white upper beak and white below — on white-sided dolphins the top of the beak is always black, white below
- pigmentation on sides and back are also useful in distinguishing two species

Identification of stranded animals

- known to be entrapped in groups in ice
- best characteristic for separating white-beaks from white-sides is the pigmentation of the head and beak
- white-beaked dolphins have 22-28 teeth per side per jaw
- white-sided dolphins have 30-40 teeth per side per jaw

Distribution and Abundance

Generally, white-beaked dolphins have a slightly more northerly distribution than do white-sided dolphins, although their ranges overlap. They are common especially in Labrador waters in summer. Because of ice entrapments, it is known that some winter in the Gulf of St. Lawrence and on the northeast coast. There are few reliable estimates of their numbers, although a census in 1982 off Labrador estimated a population in that area of about 3,000 animals. Although a few white-beaks are incidently caught in fishing nets, there is a small inshore hunt for them in parts of Labrador, and northern Newfoundland.

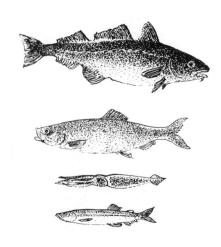

Natural History

There is little known about the biology of this dolphin. What is known has largely come from animals obtained from ice entrapments. On several occasions groups of animals have been forced inshore by pack ice until they strand. In 1983, heavy ice on the northeast coast entrapped a total of about 400 animals in many separate areas. White-beaks apparently spend winters offshore near ice and have evolved senses and abilities to cope with ice. In 1983 about 20 percent of dolphins trapped in ice died.

Data obtained from the dead animals has enabled biologists to understand more about this species.

The mortality of ice stranded animals has been minimized by the efforts of local people to stabilize the ice and help the animals. Sam Masters of Fairhaven, Placentia Bay once found a white-beak dolphin caught in ice. Failing to find any open water for the dolphin in Placentia Bay, he loaded it into the back of his truck, hauled it over to ice-free Trinity Bay, and released it.

In 1982, fishermen Eric Pretty and his crew from Dildo, Trinity Bay rescued a group of white-beaks by holding ice away from the animals with nets. With ice all around, the fishermen watched the animals carefully and observed them feeding. Most of the animals were released when the ice receded. An American aquarium purchased some of the dolphins for display.

Food for white-beaks consists mainly of squid, herring, capelin and cod. Stranded animals found around Newfoundland also had trawl lines and rocks in their stomachs.

The large schools which are sometimes reported are probably composed of several more compact social groups of 5-25 animals. This school size is more commonly seen in inshore waters from June to November. Groups may be composed of animals of different ages; some groups containing only non-mature small animals, others containing mature animals and their offspring. Calves of about 80 lbs. (35 kg) are born after a 10 month gestation.

An ice-stranded white-beaked dolphin

Common Dolphin *(Delphinus delphis)*

Common names: Saddleback dolphin

Identification

- seen offshore in large groups of 50 to several hundred animals
- very fast swimmers
- often seen breaching and playing in the bow and wake waves of ships
- mature animals 6-8 ft. (2-5 m)
- males slightly larger than females
- black, V-shaped saddle with downward point directly below dorsal fin most useful field mark
- distinct "hourglass" pattern on sides
- the forward region tan or yellow, the posterior half grey
- prominent dorsal fin triangular
- fin varies from all black to grey-white
- long, pointed beak, black eye mask
- black stripe from flipper to jaw distinctive

Identification of stranded animals

- black saddle, eyemask, and jawstripe most distinctive
- not known to mass strand
- 40-55 teeth per side per jaw

Distribution and Abundance

Common dolphins occur worldwide in the warmer waters of all oceans. In the northwest Atlantic they range from the Gulf of Mexico to Newfoundland. They are offshore animals, generally found along the edge of the continental shelf, in deep waters.

Natural History

These dolphins are very gregarious, feeding and travelling in herds numbering many hundreds. The biology of this species has been studied most extensively in the Pacific.

Most adults are 7.5 ft. (2.3m) long and weigh about 155 lbs. (75 kg). Calves about 30 inches (80 cm) long are born after a gestation period of 11 months. Common dolphins reach maturity at about 3-4 years and may live up to 30 years.

These dolphins are best known for their bow-riding antics and aerial acrobatics. Look for them at sea off the Grand Banks, where they feed primarily on fish and squid. They will often stay with a vessel for long periods and have even been known to ride the bow waves of large whales!

Beluga Whale *(Delphinapterus leucas)*
Common names: White Whale, Sea Canary

Identification

- extralimital sightings of single animals or small groups
- infrequent around Labrador and rare near the Island
- seen in groups of 3-15
- seasonally in larger groups when in normal range
- maximum overall length is 16 ft. (5m) — commonly 11-13 ft (3.5-4 m)
- most distinctive identifying mark is all white body colour — absence of a dorsal fin
- rounded bulbous forehead
- distinct 'neck' line
- robust body shape
- flippers are relatively small and well-forward
- no dorsal fin — instead a narrow ridge composed of small bumps
- newborn calves (5 ft., 1.5 m) are brown
- gradually they lighten in color and become white by their 6-7th year
- on surfacing swim slowly, blowing several times a minute
- blows tend to be inconspicuous
- dives last 5-15 minutes

Identification of stranded animals

- most positive traits are the color and absence of a dorsal fin

Distribution and Abundance

Belugas are found in shallow arctic and subarctic waters. Frequently, they are also found in rivers and estuaries. At least five separate populations are thought to inhabit the Canadian Arctic and maximum estimates of numbers are from 24,000-28,000. Beluga whales live throughout the year in the St. Lawrence River.

On the island, sightings of belugas are quite uncommon, although they have occurred in a variety of locations. Labrador sightings are more common, but are mostly north of Nain. Groups of white whales have been seen off Cape White Handkerchief and Eclipse Channel in Northern Labrador. There are no reliable estimates of numbers of beluga whales in our waters but sightings even in Northern Labrador waters have been in the low hundreds.

White whales are presently hunted in Canada's Arctic. Approximately 400-600 are killed annually. Muktuk (the skin and thin layer of blubber) is the most prized portion of the animal although the meat is also utilized.

Natural History

Sexual maturity is attained between 6-10 years of age. Males average 14 ft. (4.5m) to a maximum of 16 ft. (5m). Females average 13 ft. (4m). Average adult weights range from about 900 lbs. (400 kg) for females to 1,400 lbs. (640 kg) for males. Maximum weights for either sex are about double average weights. Conception occurs in early May. After a gestation period of 14.5 months, a 100 lb. (45 kg) calf is born. Nursing continues for about one year or longer. On average a female beluga becomes pregnant about every 3 years. Extreme ages are from 25-30 years; after about 20-21 years of age females rarely become pregnant.

Belugas usually are found in fairly shallow waters and feed along the bottom. In general they dive up to 125 ft. (40m) to find food which includes about 50 lbs. (25 kg) per day of squid, crabs, shrimp, clams and fish.

Vocalizations by belugas are frequent and complex, designed to fit their active social lives. Their frequent whistles earned them the name 'sea canary'. They also produce click sounds used in echolocation, 'bell' sounds, and loud claps made by snapping their jaws together.

Social organization consists of small groups of whales which may be either harem groups or all male groups. During the breeding season and migrations, smaller groups merge.

The behaviour of animals sighted around Newfoundland often appears quite abnormal. One female with a calf sighted for several weeks around St. John's became caught in a codtrap and died; her calf disappeared. In another case, fisherman Donald Wagner of Harbor Breton was approached by a single white whale. The animal rubbed against the boat and allowed itself to be petted. Thinking it was hungry, fishermen gave it herring, which it would take in its mouth but would not swallow. After an hour, the fishermen headed home, followed by the white whale.

Narwhal *(Monodon monoceros)*

Common name: Unicorn whale

Identification

- an arctic whale rarely seen in Newfoundland waters
- on occasion seen off Labrador in summer months
- usually seen in groups of 10 or more
- sightings and strandings in Newfoundland have been only of single individuals
- narwhals reach a maximum length of 16 ft. (5m)
- mature males are easily identified by a long tusk (up to 10 ft., 3m)
- tusk grows from the front left of the upper jaw
- females seldom have tusks
- immature males may have short tusks
- tusks have spiral twist
- head is blunt — body is cylindrical
- young animals are dark grey
- with age, animals develop numerous spots over back
- underside is light
- no dorsal fin on back
- a series of low bumps may be visible on lower back

Identification of stranded animals

- most positive trait is the tusk (in males)
- tusk develops from one of the two teeth in the upper jaw
- absence of dorsal fin and coloration are also useful

Abundance and Distribution

The narwhal is common in eastern Canadian Arctic waters and off Greenland. In winter, it migrates to the south edge of pack ice in Davis Strait as well as to Disco Bay off West Greenland. Northern migration occurs in spring into Baffin Bay. Because they are a migratory, deep water species, narwhals are hard to count. It is estimated that there may be as many as 20,000-30,000 animals.

There is a hunt for narwhals in Canadian waters by Inuits, centred primarily on north Baffin Island. Including the annual catch in West Greenland, 500-600 animals per year may be killed. The animals are used for muktuk and the tusks sell for $75-$100 per kg.

Sightings in Labrador are uncommon; sightings in Newfoundland are rare and extralimital.

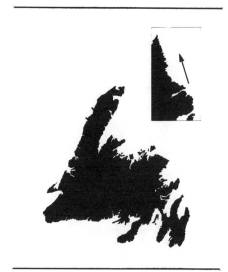

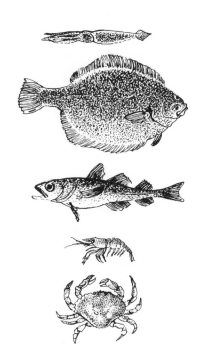

Natural History

The age of sexual maturity in the narwhal is believed to be about five years for females and 8-9 years for males. Breeding occurs about mid-April and gestation lasts about 14.5 months. Calves produced in mid-July weigh about 180 lbs. (80 kg) at birth. Lactation lasts for 18-20 months. An average 15-16 ft. (4.7m) male is about 1.8 tons (1,600 kg). Females average about 13 ft. (4m) and weigh about 1 ton (900 kg).

The tusk of the male narwhal is the most famous aspect of this whale. It is probably used in inter-male competition, and to attract females. There is some evidence for aggressive use of the tusk, but other uses have been suggested as well, including capture of prey, opening holes in ice, digging in the bottom mud, as a cooling mechanism, and as a defensive weapon.

Food of the narwhal consists of squid, crabs, shrimp and fish. Most commonly it seems to eat Arctic cod and flatfish.

Narwhals use a variety of frequent vocalizations to maintain social organization and to orient to objects. Echolocation clicks, whistles and several lower frequency vocalizations have been recorded. Narwhals are probably polygamous, where one male breeds with several females during a breeding season, although relatively little is known of their social organization.

From March to April, 1978, a young male narwhal shared a small area of open water, surrounded by ice, with four humpback whales, directly off the city of Springdale. During its stay, the small narwhal tolerated its large, strange companions and the great deal of public attention it received very well. When an icebreaker opened a channel so the animals could escape to open water, it was last seen swimming away to sea with the humpbacks.

NOT A WHALE!

Basking Shark *(Cetorhinus maximus)*

Basking sharks have often been confused with whales, probably because of their large size. They are not whales though; they are the second largest fish in the world (second only to the whale shark). A mature shark can be over 30 feet (10m) long and weigh up to 4 tons (about 4,000 kg). Their huge bodies are slate-gray in colour and they have 5 enormously long gill openings that stretch around their necks. You would most likely see them swimming at the surface with their large, triangular dorsal fins approximately 3 ft. (1m) high, and often the tips of their tail fins breaking the surface. The other place where you might encounter basking sharks is hauled up at the wharf in any of the fishing villages along the south coast, the Avalon Peninsula, and the northeast coast, from June to September.

Basking sharks seem to move inshore when waters warm to above 80⁰C to satisfy feeding and reproductive needs. This shark feeds generally on plankton, copepods, amphipods and euphausiids. Unlike most sharks, the basking shark has many tiny teeth that are only about 5mm long. It feeds in a very unique way by sieving plankton out of the water.

The long gill openings extend almost completely around the neck allowing a huge volume of water to flow through them. Each opening has a gill arch with thousands of gill-rakers attached to it. These gill-rakers are fine, comb-like structures that the shark uses to strain and filter plankton from the water. The shark swims with its mouth open (about 3 ft./1m across when open) through a concentration of plankton and sieves out food with its gill-rakers. The water then passes out through the gill openings. This feeding method is similar to the skimming method the right whale uses with its baleen plates.

It is intriguing to note that sharks evolved approximately 400 million years ago (200 million years before the first dinosaurs walked on earth). Whales have only been in their present form for about 25 million years. Yet both groups contain a species that feeds in very much the same manner — the basking shark and the right whale.

Little is known about reproduction in the basking shark. We do know the male has large, modified pelvic fins called claspers, which place the sperm packets within the female's vagina, ensuring internal fertilization. The large whale shark, the closest relative to the basking shark, is known to lay eggs. The basking shark (like the dogfish shark) may bear live young, although this has never been proven. The female has many internal structures called trophonemata whose sole purpose is to secrete nourishment for the live young. Also the gland necessary to produce an eggshell is very small in the basking shark, yet it is highly developed in the whale shark.

In the summer of 1983, a 23 ft. (7m) female shark that had recently copulated was found, providing for the first time direct evidence of inshore sexual activity by basking sharks in Newfoundland waters.

After they depart our waters in the autumn, basking sharks are believed to spend the winter in the deep waters of the Gulf of St. Lawrence (especially the Laurentian Channel), where they are occasionally caught by trawlers. Winter strays have been found with no gill-rakers at all. There is a theory that they shed their gill-rakers, stop feeding, sink to the bottom and hibernate. While they are inactive they grow new rakers for the next spring.

Entrapment Problems

These huge, harmless, slow moving sharks blunder into nets, often totally destroying the fishing gear. They tear gigantic holes in nets and their rough hide often chafes the lines and ropes to the breaking point. basking shark damage to fishing gear.

Ninety-five percent of all basking shark damage to fishing gear was done to salmon nets, with codtraps and gill nets also being damaged. There is currently a market for certain shark parts and this helps to compensate the fisherman for damage to his gear and livelihood. One fisherman in 1983 lost 10 salmon nets in 6 weeks due to sharks, and could not possibly repair them or resume fishing. In the past the salmon fishery accounted for about 30-50 percent of most southwest coast fishermen's annual incomes.

A young basking shark filter feeding near a gill net

The basking shark's liver, which can weigh up to one ton (25 percent of the fish's total body weight), can be removed and rendered into oil. An 1800 lb. (820 kg) liver may yield 600 gallons (2270 litres) of oil. The oil was used in lamps before petroleum was discovered, and was also a supplementary source of Vitamin A (similar to cod liver oil). Presently the oil is used for lubrication in machinery and as a base for some cosmetics. The liver was valued at 55¢/kg in 1983.

The large fins are also utilized and sold for $1.90/kg in 1983. They are dried and shipped to Hong Kong and the Orient to be used in the Chinese delicacy, shark fin soup.

Further uses for the hide, flesh, stomach contents and cartilage of this huge fish are being researched. As of yet an efficient means of protecting fishing gear from the sharks has not been found.

Harp seals

Introducing Seals

There are three main divisions of pinnipeds; the true seals (phocidae), the walrus (odobenidae) and the sealions and fur seals (otariidae - both eared seals). There are 34 species of seals world-wide. This guide will deal with 6 species of true seals found in Newfoundland and Labrador waters, and the walrus which occasionally strays this way. Eared seals do not occur in the North Atlantic.

The true seals have sleek, compact bodies with flipper-like fore-limbs. Their hind-limbs are used for propulsion in swimming but are useless for walking on land. Therefore, when on land, they use a caterpillar-hitch movement, much like an inchworm. Since progress on land is rather awkward, it is rare to find seals far from the sea where they are most at home.

These seals give birth on specific breeding grounds and then mate after the pups are weaned. Most females have only one pup although twins have been reported. For reproduction some seals form pairs. In other species, mating occurs in groups with dominant, territorial males fathering the most pups.

Seals are carnivorous, opportunistic eaters, feeding on a wide variety of fish, mollusks and crustacea. They usually eat 6-10 percent of their body weight each day. Their weight will fluctuate seasonally — for example, ringed seals will show a weight gain of 31-34 percent in the winter and a weight loss of 18-30 percent in the spring.

Seals are known for their ability to dive to considerable depths and stay submerged. They have remarkable breathing and circulatory adaptations that enable them to do this. Dives to 940 ft. (300m) have been recorded for hooded seals who can decrease their heartbeat from 100 beats/minute to 10 beats/minute and stay down for up to 18 minutes.

The main predator of seals throughout history has been man. Seals are hunted for their fur, blubber (for oil), and meat.

Seal Sighting

Unlike whales, which are usually glimpsed only momentarily while blowing or diving, seals can often be seen resting in full view. This gives the observer a much better chance to identify the animal. Many species are highly social and haul-outs of hundreds of animals may be seen, especially during moulting. Again viewing conditions can vary greatly and distance, weather and sea-state all affect how much information you can obtain to determine the species.

Seals typically observe a daily pattern; they haul out at dawn, return to sea at dusk and feed at night. Good times of day to view them are about half-way through the haul-out period, around noon. Mid-low tide would be your best chance if there are tidal restrictions in the area.

Seals on land are very skittish, and almost always head for the water at the first sign of human activity. Sneaking up on seals takes patience and practice! Stay low to the ground, and downwind. On cloudy days seals seem more wary, as their vision is poorer with less light. On sunny days, they are more likely to sleep soundly and are easier to approach. During moulting season, seals generally haul out in larger groups and seem less susceptible to disturbances. Seals in the water will often show great curiosity for humans and boats, and may approach quite closely.

In the spring if you overly disturb the seals a mother may desert her pup. Even if a pup appears to be alone its mother may be close by, so do not pet or handle it.

Ho! We be the sealers of Newfoundland!
We clear from a snowy shore,
Out into the gale with our steam and sail,
Where tempest and tumult roar.
We battle the floe as we northward go,
North, from a frozen strand!
Through lead, through bay, we fight our way,
We sealers of Newfoundland!

George Allan England
The Sealers of Newfoundland

The Seal Hunt

Northern people have hunted seals as a way of life for centuries. Such hunts provided the essentials of food and clothing. Commercial sealing evolved from the development of oil, leather and fur markets and was directed at the breeding concentrations of primarily harp but also hooded seals.

In Newfoundland and Labrador and the Gulf, the sealing industry was well established and flourishing by the early 18th century. Fishermen earned about half of their yearly income from the sale of harp seal skins and oil during that period. In the 19th century schooners were introduced and the heyday of the seal hunt bloomed from 1825-1860, with a maximum catch of 744,000 seals in 1832. Steam and steel ships with icebreaker bows and radios followed, all of which made the hunt more effective and safer for the sealers. During the World Wars of this century the hunt was discontinued and depleted herds had an opportunity to increase. After the war, the hunt began again, rejuvenated by foreign investment and diesel vessels.

Canadian scientists started studying the harp seal stocks in 1951. Much information was needed for proper biological management of these populations. Previous exploitation of harp seals was based on economics and opportunity, without a clear understanding of the impact of man's activities on the population. There was a need for regulation of the hunt and conservation of the harp seal population. Regulations were first introduced in 1961, when May 5 was set aside as a closing date for the hunt. Numbers of harp seals, however, continued to decline with an average annual catch of about 287,000 animals per year. Reduction in stock size between 1950 and 1970 was about 50 percent, from 2.5-3.0 million animals to approximately 1.5 million animals. In 1971 an annual quota system was introduced which limited the number of animals that could be taken. Quota controls were tightened throughout the 1970s and extended to landsmen. Even though marine animals are difficult to census and there have been gaps in the data and varying interpretation, the best evidence since 1982 suggests that the northwest Atlantic harp seal population is increasing. Continued and careful monitoring of the population is still essential.

While depletion of any population of animals exploited by man is a legitimate reason for concern and action, arguments that the harp seal is presently headed for extinction are not supported by scientific fact. There are, however, legitimate questions of value raised about our annual seal hunt. These include the question of humane killing and utilization of the animals.

There are two categories of seal hunting: (1) large vessels which hunt in the Gulf and at the Front for whitecoats primarily and (2) landsmen that hunt from shore using fairly small boats. Adult seals are shot with rifles by landsmen and whitecoats are clubbed. In recent years, through a licensing program, participants in seal hunting have been controlled and the killing is monitored by scientists and enforcement officials. Killing methods are also regulated. The death of any living creature cannot be made appealing. There are extensive data which indicate the clubbing method of killing whitecoats is humane and comparable with North American slaughterhouse standards. There is less data on the efficiency of killing by rifles in the landsmen's hunt.

The final question concerning the seal hunt has been the use of the dead animal. Some object to the fact that furs are used for trivial purposes, such as in fashion, when there are substitutes. Others object to the fact that all of the meat is not used by man for food because of poor markets. Markets and their fluctuations are largely outside any possible control by sealers themselves; they are simply primary producers supplying seals for the price offered. Arguments over values are emotionally charged and debate on the comparative value of what to eat or wear will undoubtedly continue; it may be difficult to agree on a set of values that will suit everyone.

There's a noble fleet of sealers,
Being fitted for the ice,
They'll take a chance again this year
tho' fat's gone down in price.
And the owners will supply them
as in the days of old,
For in Newfoundland the Sealing Voyage
means something more than gold.

And now they're back in old St. John's.
A-sharing out the flippers,
Let's wish good luck to sealers all
Likewise their gallant skippers.
Tho' Newfoundland is changing fast
Some things we must not lose,
May we always have our flipper pie,
And codfish for our brewis.

Gerald S. Doyle collection

We Sealers of Newfoundland

Mark Small is President of the Sealers' Association. Mark has been sealing as a landsman for 12-15 years in the White Bay area.

"My father was a fisherman. He fished summers and sealed in the winter-time. There were 6 boys and 5 girls in the family. The 6 boys grew up and we're all fishermen. We've got 6 longliners. All these boats cost anywhere from $50,000 to $650,000.

"In my father's day, well, it was different. We're a class of businessmen. We have commitments to the bank, because we've invested hundreds of thousands of dollars into the fishery. They didn't have commitments. If they got bread and butter to go on the table for the family, well, that was fine.

"That was their way of life. Our way of life has changed. You've got to have the latest technology to go out and fish. Since the 200 mile limit, there's been a significant increase in the fishery. There's a lot of people who have gotten into it and in a big way. We need the seal fishery. We need the cod fishery. We need everything we can get just to survive.

"Now there's two aspects to the seal fishery — the landsmen and the offshore sealers. The offshore sealers used to go out on ships to the ice and harvest white-coats. Clubbing is only done by the offshore sealers.

"I'm a landsman. We usually travel off the land in our boats, our longliners. We've developed a fleet of longliners capable of going offshore 60 miles. The major sealing area is from Fogo north to Belle Isle. We usually don't go any farther north than Bell Isle.

"With the kind of sealing I'm involved in we shoot the seal. He just puts his head up through the water and we shoot them. They're instantly killed. They've got a good chance to escape.

"The federal government has very strict regulations on the seal hunt. You have to have a certain high-powered rifle. You have to make sure there is no life, and you have to skin the seal right. The Fisheries officers come out to the ice and do an inspection to see that you've got the right gun, a proper gaff, and your licence on you. I think that's the way it should be. You don't have non-professionals who don't know what they're doing into the seal fishery.

"Right now to start you go out on the boat with a professional sealer for one season and you go through a training period. Then the next season you apply for a beginner's licence.

"In the offshore sealing you must club the seal at least three times. I think the clubbing is humane. Studies have shown it is one of the most humane ways of killing an animal. For instance it is instantly rendered unconscious from the first blow. The Fisheries officers see that you kill it humanely and follow their directions to the letter. And if you don't, they take your licence from you.

"The offshore fishermen did not usually take the young carcasses because there's not much meat on a white-coat. They do take the flippers though. We landsmen bring in all our meat and sell the carcasses. At that time it's a beater seal and there's more meat on the carcass.

"I usually bottle up some seal meat and we have a few flippers in our freezer, probably a couple of carcasses of young seal too. People come around summer-time to visit and they like seal meat. We'll open probably a bottle of seal or a flipper you know.

"Europe was the main market — France, Germany and England. But because of the protest groups and the moral issue of clubbing seals it turned the people off and now they don't buy the product. We know that it is an image problem. This white-coat business is very emotional.

"Still our biggest aim is to change public opinion, to re-educate the people. One of the most effective ways I can think of to change public opinion is for the public to see me, or some other sealer from around Newfoundland, who depends on the seal fishery for his living.

"If a man uses the resources wisely then they'll always be there. Look, I'd be one of the first ones to say put a ban on the seal hunt if I knew the species was endangered, but it's not."

Key to Seals

Key features to note when you first spot a seal are its relative size and the shape of its head. Use the key to the seals to narrow down your choices. Other clues to notice are whether the animals are sighted in small or large groups and whether they are on ice, in water, or on land. Once you have a general idea of what species you are seeing, turn to that section for key identification and comparison information.

Some of the seals in our waters have been tagged by scientists studying the animals. Usually hind flipper ribbons or tags are used. If you see a tagged seal, record the colour of the tag, its number, and when and where you spotted the animal. This information is useful to scientists to help them identify individuals, census the population and trace migration patterns. Send any records to Dr. Deane Renouf, Memorial University, St. John's, Nfld. A1B 3X9, or to Fisheries and Oceans, P.O. Box 5667, St. John's.

In learning to identify the different species of seals your knowledge of their habits and life histories can increase as well. This type of public knowledge and awareness is the backbone of sound management and conservation of these unique marine mammals.

Seal Sightings Locations

Newfoundland

1. Chance Cove
2. Red Island
   (Southwest Cove)
3. Green Island and
   Little Green Island
4. Miquelon (on the Dunes)
5. Brunette Island
   (Mercer Cove)
6. Sagoni Island
7. Pass Island

Labrador

1. Lake Melville
2. Okak Islands — and all along the coast north of Nain

From February through March seals are found on the pack ice from Northern Labrador to Southern Newfoundland.

Comparison of head shape and size

Bearded seal

Hood seal

Gray seal

Harp seal

Harbour seal

Ring seal

Harp Seal *(Phoca groenlandica)*
Common names: Harp, Whitecoat, Raggedy Jackets, Beaters, Bedlamers, Kairulik

Identification

- seasonally abundant off Newfoundland and Labrador and Gulf of St. Lawrence
- in spring, seen in large groups on ice, as seals congregate to pup and mate
- migrate and feed in loose groups of up to several hundred
- may be very lively, leaping and playing in small groups
- adults average length is 5.5 ft. (1.7m)
- head is small in relation to body
- pointed nose, low sloping forehead, large eyes
- head dark in colour
- coloration is basically light white or tan with dark patches
- in adults dark patches produce black horse-shoe shaped band or 'harp' on the
- back and sides
- males show the most pronounced harp
- females have paler harp and head
- newborn pups (to two weeks) are snow white (whitecoats)
- this coat partially moulted from 2-4 weeks (raggedy jackets)
- yearlings fully moulted have short silvery coat with dark spots along side and
- back (beaters) and are in the water
- immature harps with spotted coat more than one year old (bedlamers)

Identification of dead animals

- if coat is intact, most positive trait on adults is presence of harp

opposite — A white coat with its mother on the ice

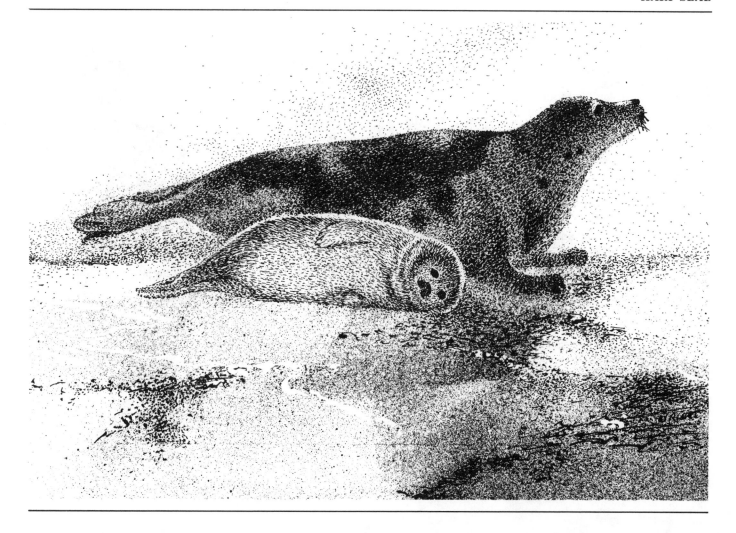

Distribution and Abundance

The world-wide distribution of harp seals is based on three widely-separated breeding populations: (1) northwest Atlantic, primarily the northeast coast of Newfoundland, southeast coast of Labrador and the Gulf of St. Lawrence; (2) White Sea; (3)Jan Mayer Island in the Arctic Ocean. The White Sea and Jan Mayer populations exchange some individuals. These populations are similar and probably distinct from the population around Newfoundland.

Harps migrate north in the spring, following the pack ice and migrate south in the fall ahead of the new ice. In the annual migration the seals must swim over 3,200 km to reach the Arctic waters.

Presently the number of harp seals totals 1.6-2.3 million animals. The northwest Atlantic population contains about 1.0-1.5 million animals. Historical estimates of the numbers of harp seals are somewhat higher. The northwest Atlantic population is not considered endangered and by best current population estimates the population is increasing.

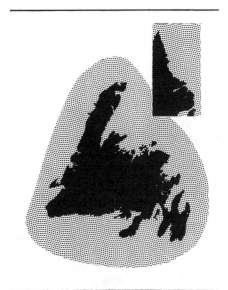

right — the harp shape is clearly visible on the adult coat

Male and female on the ice
top right — Male with hood inflated

Hooded Seal *(Cystophora cristata)*
Common names: Hood, Bladdernose, Blueback, Netsivak

Identification

- common near edge of pack ice from Newfoundland to Davis Strait
- solitary except during the mating season in April and May
- large herds are formed in mating season
- large seal — 9-10 ft. long (2.7-3m)
- weight between 400-725 lbs. (180-330 kg)
- males (dogs), are larger than females
- the head of males is unusual, a hood-like sac on top of the muzzle
- can be inflated in the form of a large crest
- also an inflatable red nasal membrane through which they can blow out
- one nostril much like a balloon
- coats of adults are distinctive blue-grey in colour — covered in dark,
- uneven blotches
- face is solid black
- blotches less distinctive in water and when wet
- pups ("bluebacks") have silver grey coat with cream-white belly

Identification of dead animals

- most positive traits are the size, coloration and presence of hood on males
- skull has very short cranium with long, wide snout compared with other seals

Natural History

In Canadian waters, pregnant cows haul out onto the pack ice in late February or early March. The population divides into two main herds. One herd is found on the southward drifting ice off Labrador (the Front); the second occurs in the Gulf of St. Lawrence near the Magdalen Islands. Once on the ice the herd forms several main 'patches' which vary from 20-200 km² and consist of densities up to 2,000 females per km².

Pups when born are about 3 ft. (1m) in length, weighing 25 lbs. (10 kg) and are yellow in colour. At about three days their fur turns white. Pups are nursed for 9-12 days and then abandoned. During the brief nursing period the pups easily triple in weight. This short concentrated lactation and fast pup growth is an adaptation to the unstable ice environment. Conditions suitable for nursing can change rapidly as ice breaks up or rafts unexpectedly.

About two weeks after whelping, the adults mate. Males reach sexual maturity between 7-8 years; females mature between 4-6 years of age. Gestation is approximately 11.5 months but, for about three months, development of the embryo is virtually suspended. This delay in development ensures that birthing occurs at about the same time each year, just when the ice conditions are right.

In early April harp seals moult. During the month spent replacing their old coat they do not feed. On completion of moulting, they begin a northward migration to their Arctic feeding grounds. This completes the cycle performed annually by harp seals for each of their 35 or more years.

During the winter, harps feed mainly on capelin, but also take herring, polar cod and redfish. In the summer months arctic cod is the staple food, along with sea snails, sculpins, Greenland halibut and eelpouts. Young seals feed mostly on small crustacea (euphausiids). Food habits during migrations are less well known, but it appears the seals eat less during these periods. To find food such as groundfish, the harp seal can dive to depths of 640 ft. (200m). Dive times are variable but can last from 2-15 minutes. After a dive the animal returns to the surface to breath and may spend 5 minutes before diving again.

Fifteen underwater sounds have been recorded from harp seals, including grunts, squeaks and clicks. They possess excellent eyesight underwater, although it is poor in air, especially in low light levels. Their hearing is also adapted for underwater, but is still very good in air.

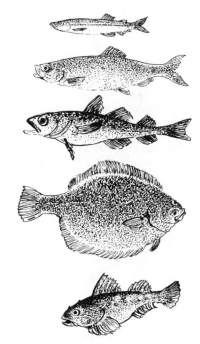

Distribution and Abundance

The hooded seal is normally found only in the North Atlantic. This population is estimated to be in the range of 300,000-400,000 animals and is found from Lancaster Sound east to the Denmark Straits and south to the Gulf of St. Lawrence. There are three major herds in: (1) Davis Strait; (2) Newfoundland including the Gulf; (3) Jan Mayen Island. All herds tend to follow a similar annual migration. The entire population assembles each summer between mid-June to mid-July in a moulting area on pack ice in the Denmark Strait.

In late August, the seals disperse widely to feed, primarily in deep Greenland waters. Winter pack ice forces them south and many feed off the Grand Banks. In February, adults begin to assemble in the three major whelping areas.

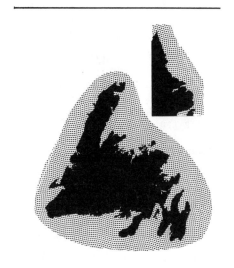

Natural History

Pups, born on offshore ice during the last half of March, weigh about 60 lbs. (27 kg) and are about 3 ft. (1m) long. Adult males wait on the ice until the end of the 7-12 day nursing period, displaying vigorous courtship, inflating their hoods and red nasal sacs, and vocalizing loudly. Battles are common. Copulation occurs at the end of lactation. Very slow initial development of the embryo ensures that gestation lasts about 11.5 months, so each year's birthing will occur in proper ice conditions. Hoods mature at 2-6 years and may live to about 35 years of age

Hooded seals are excellent divers; a month-old pup descended to 240 ft. (75m) on its very first dive! They seem to prefer open, deep water and drift ice and are seldom seen near shore. Their diet consists mostly of squid, redfish and herring, although capelin, cod and mussels are also eaten. Adults eat about 55 lbs. (30 kg) per day but fast when breeding and moulting.

Hoods and harp seals occur and breed in many of the same areas, and so have traditionally been hunted together. Hoods prefer to whelp on rough, heavy ice, while harps prefer thin smooth ice near the water's edge. Hooded seals whelp about a week later than harps so they are hunted towards the end of the harp seal hunt.

The main object of the commercial hood seal hunt is the blueback, which is the most desirable seal pelt. Unlike harps, adult hooded seals defend their pups fiercely and are dangerous. In 1977 the total hooded seal quota was set at 15,000 animals. In 1979 new regulations stated that sealers could only kill female hoods if it was in self-defence. The maximum limit on them was set at 5 per cent of the total catch. In the absence of reliable estimates of the size of the Newfoundland herd, it is difficult to evaluate the impact of hunting. Currently a census effort is underway by Fisheries and Oceans Canada.

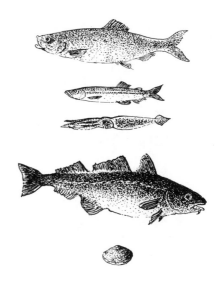

Harbour Seal *(Phoca vitulina concolor)*

Common names: Common Seal, Spotted Seal, Kassigak
Dodder (adult), Ranger (immature)

Identification

- common throughout Newfoundland and southern Labrador waters
- typically seen near shore
- may be resting close to mainland on islands
- usually alone in the water
- when resting, may be seen in small groups
- adults 5-6 ft. (1.5-1.8 m) — maximum weight 250 lbs. (115 kg)
- small head, large eyes
- short muzzle — nostrils form broad 'V' shape
- very stout, cylindrical body
- basic coat colour varies from light grey to tan, to even reddish-brown
- with dark spots
- spots are smaller and fewer on underside
- coat colour in water appears darker, and dark spots may not be visible
- daily habits are usually tied to the tidal cycle — haul out on ledges to rest and bask at low tide — disperse and hunt for food at high tide

Identification of dead animals

- body traits previously described will help

WRIGHT '82

Distribution and Abundance

Harbour seals have one of the most widespread distributions, inhabiting most seas and even land-locked lakes. There are a number of subspecies worldwide; world population is roughly estimated between 750,000-1,000,000 animals. The eastern North American subspecies is called *Phoca vitulina concolor*. It occurs in scattered numbers from Greenland to the central and eastern Arctic and along the eastern seaboard. Harbour seals are nonmigratory and are believed to overwinter in locations where currents maintain open water. There are no reliable estimates of numbers for the Canadian Arctic, the east coat or Newfoundland and Labrador waters.

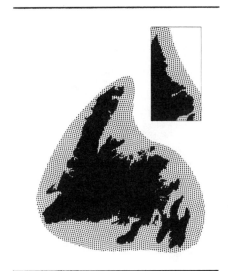

Natural History

The birth season lasts one to ten days occurring between April and June in northwest Atlantic coastal waters. Pups weigh about 25 lbs. (11 kg) at birth and are weaned in 3-4 weeks. Prior to birth most pups shed their whitish coat and are born with the spotted adult coat. During nursing, the mother-pup bond is very strong and when in danger mother seals have been seen to grab their pups with front flippers or mouth and dive to safety. Pups can swim at birth, and when just two days old can dive for up to two minutes. Harbour seals become sexually mature at 3-6 years. Mating takes place during the summer when courtship and sparring between males can be observed in the water near haul-out ledges. There is a sizable breeding area on the French island of Miquelon.

Harbour seals have a varied diet which includes herring, crabs, flatfish, cod and sculpin. Feeding occurs during the day; night feeding is known to occur in places where haul-out beaches are not affected by tide height. Harbour seals get about 90 per cent of the fresh water they need from preformed water in the fish they eat, from metabolic processes and also from inhaled water vapour. They drink sea water only incidentally while swallowing food.

They have lived up to 35 years in captivity; estimates on longevity in the wild are not well established. Natural mortality is caused by storms, disease, young abandonment and predation by sharks, killer whales and humans. Because of damage to fishing gear and fisheries, bounties and killings at breeding sites in many areas have occurred. No noticeable effects were seen on fish catches, however, and bounties were lifted.

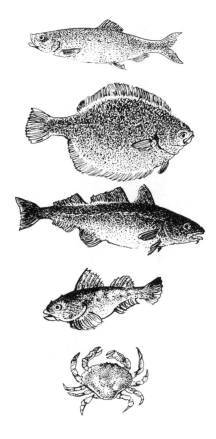

Comparison of head shapes and nostrils —

left — Harbour seal
right — Gray seal

Gray Seal *(Halichoerus grypus)*
Common names: Jar seal, Netsiak

Identification

- common in several areas of Newfoundland and Labrador
- seen in large groups during January-March breeding season
- smaller groups and individuals at other times
- sexually distinguishable — males to 8 ft. (2.4m) and 375-600 lbs. (170-300 kg)
- females to 7 ft. (2m) and 230-400 lbs. (100-180 kg)
- most obvious feature of head is a lengthened snout with wide muzzle
- general shape is that of horse or moose head without ears
- roman nose or horsehead shape is most conspicuous in males
- female's nose is more slender
- head fairly small in comparison to body
- fur coloration is variable — females often quite light in neck and dark on back
- males generally darker
- both sexes have irregular spots of light and dark
- to differentiate between gray and harbour seals in water compare relative size and examine head shape and nostrils
- gray seal has parallel slits separated by a large gap
- harbour seal has inclined slits joined at the base
- gray seals often swim "crocodile-like" with nostrils and eyes protruding slightly above the water's surface
- their exhalation is unusually loud, and can be heard over some distance
- males have massive shoulders with folded, scarred skin over chest area

Identification of dead animals

- most positive trait is the horse-head shape
- nostrils are parallel slits
- skull characterized by high, wide snout compared to other seals
- five claws are conspicuous on foreflipper

opposite — Male and female mating

Distribution and Abundance

Worldwide there are three main populations of gray seal: (1) eastern North Atlantic, (2) Baltic Sea and (3) western North Atlantic. The world population is estimated around 120,000 animals of which about 30,000 are found in Canadian waters. In recent years the number of gray seals in eastern Canada has been increasing.

Gray seals do not migrate but do travel long distances after breeding. Nine pups that were born on Sable Island were found in Conception Bay and on Miquelon, and another one got as far as Hopedale, Labrador. Probably one of the better marathon swimmers was the pup that left Sable Island and 25 days later was recovered 1,280 km away at Barnegut Light, New Jersey; an average of 50 km/day!

There is a sizable breeding population of gray seals on Sable Island. There are others on the Magdalen Islands, Amet Island and at Point Michaud on the east coast of Cape Breton Island. They also breed on shore-fast ice. Around Newfoundland, gray seals are abundant on the French island of Miquelon. In late spring and summer, grays are found along the south coast and the Southern Shore of the Avalon Peninsula with fewer animals reported on the north coasts. Along the coast of Labrador they are found particularly near Hamilton Inlet, but also in many other areas. It is not unusual for gray seals breeding on the ice in Northumberland Strait to find themselves carried by wind and currents as far as Port-aux-Basques and Codroy.

Natural History

Whelping is from January to mid-February on islands or land-fast ice. The cow nurses her pup for 16-21 days. At birth a pup weighs from 25-45 lbs. (11-20 kg) and is about 3 ft. (1m) long. It gains an average of 4 lbs. (1.8 kg) per day. A single bull mates with several cows, usually on land. The cows and bulls leave the breeding ground after mating while the pups remain another 14 days or so. Females can become pregnant between 4-5 years of age while males mature at about 8 years. In the wild, female grays may live up to 44 years while males only live up to 30 years of age. Must be tough being a gray seal male!

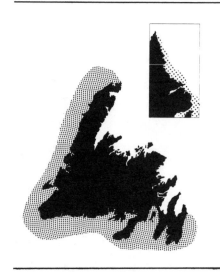

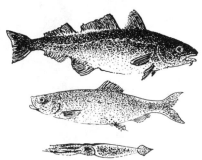

Sharks or killer whales occasionally attack gray seals but their main predator is man. Because of damage to commercial fisheries and bounties, systematic killing at breeding sites has occurred. Gray seals cause damage to fisheries by eating fish caught in nets and occasionally by damaging the gear itself. They also play a vital role in the transmission of the cod worm *(Phocanema decipiens)*. The worm larvae live in the flesh of cod which are eaten by the seal. Once eaten, the cod worm matures into an adult in the seal's stomach and reproduces. The worms are then excreted and eaten by crustacea which in turn are eaten by the codfish, so the cycle continues around again. While the cod worm occurs in other seals, it is most abundant in the gray. The worms are killed by freezing or cooking, and even though they are not dangerous, they do seriously affect the market value of commercial catches. While populations have been decreased by systematic killings, these reductions have not been clearly linked to reductions in cod worm infestation rates.

Young gray seal

Ringed Seal *(Phoca hispida hispida)*

Common names: Jar Seal, Netsiak

Identification

- common in Labrador and northern Newfoundland waters
- usually seen alone — sometimes in loose groups
- about 4 ft. (1.4m) long — males slightly larger
- weight averages about 110 lbs. (50 kg.)
- one of the smallest seals
- body round
- small head with less evidence of a neck than other species
- coloration on fur shows obvious grey-white rings on dark gray back
- silver colored belly
- pups have white woolly coat shed by 6-8 weeks
- always show preference for ice
- seen swimming among ice floes in summer, in leads in fall

Identification of dead animals

- most positive traits are small size and presence of ringed coloration on
- back with light belly

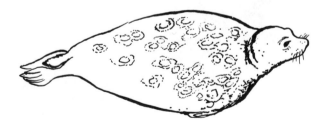

Distribution and Abundance

The ringed seal is the most numerous and widely distributed marine animal in the Arctic. They are most abundant in coastal regions because of their need for stable land-fast ice. In eastern Canada they extend from the Arctic Ocean south to northern Newfoundland. In Labrador there is a population in Lake Melville, but the greatest concentration is in northern Labrador. Minimum world-wide population is estimated at 2.5 million animals. Numbers in the Canadian Arctic are estimated to be over 500,000 animals.

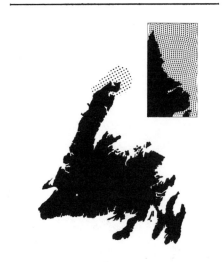

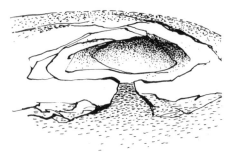

The birth lair of a ringed seal

Arctic fox

Natural History

Sexual maturity is attained by males from 6-10 years of age with most becoming mature in their seventh year. Many females are mature by their sixth year, and all by their seventh year. Pups are born in unique birth lairs hollowed out of snowdrifts in the lee of pressure ridges and hummocks. They are built on fast ice from the last half of March to the first half of April. The lairs probably serve to protect the pup from weather rather than from predators. The pup nurses for 3-8 weeks depending partially on the ice stability. Pups are born with a completely erupted set of permanent teeth.

The breeding season extends from March to May and copulation occurs in water under ice. Virtually nothing is known about the social organization of ringed seals. Ringed seals produce four types of vocalizations which are heard through the year. The average lifespan for a ringed seal is about 15-20 years, although a maximum age of 43 years has been recorded.

Their varied diet consists of Arctic cod and related fish as well as large zooplankton, shrimps and crustacea. About 11-13 lbs. (5-6 kg) of food is required daily. There is seasonal cycle of feeding with little feeding occurring during moulting. As winter progresses and the ice thickens, ringed seals keep their breathing holes open by continual use and by clawing the ice with their front flippers. Dives may be up to 45 minutes in length.

Inuit experiences in hunting ringed seals show that they have exceptional hearing and vision. They are very difficult to sneak up on!

Arctic foxes prey on seal pups and polar bears hunt adults on the offshore ice. Ringed seals have traditionally been hunted by the Inuit of Canada, Alaska, Greenland and Siberia. Between 1960-1970 Alaskan Eskimos took approximately 10,000 animals. In Labrador, the ringed seal is the most abundant year round seal and has replaced the harp seal as the main prey of coastal residents. The annual harvest on the Labrador coast and in Lake Melville from 1972-1979 was between 1,150 and 3,125 animals.

Bearded seal *(Erignathus barbatus)*

Common names: Square flipper, singing seal, Oogruk or Ugjuk, Lassies

Identification

- seen in Labrador in association with moving pack ice
- most often seen singly on ice floes
- hauled out beside escape hole or lead
- usually a solitary animal — does not form herds
- the largest of the arctic seals — 7.5 ft. (2.3m) long — weighs about 500 lbs. (230 kg)
- head unusually small for massive body
- long, bushy moustache of yellowish bristles
- coloration is uniform light to dark grey fur
- some tan to brown variations
- pups dark brown with a distinctive light face mask, and 1 to 4 light bands across head and back
- blunt, square fore flipper
- very vocal underwater — can often be heard but not seen in open water — ice areas
- songs are heard from March-July and consist of long, wavering warbles followed by short low moans

Identification of dead animals

- small head with bristle moustache and large body
- blunt fore flippers –– third digit is longest — on other seals first digit is longest
- uniform coloration

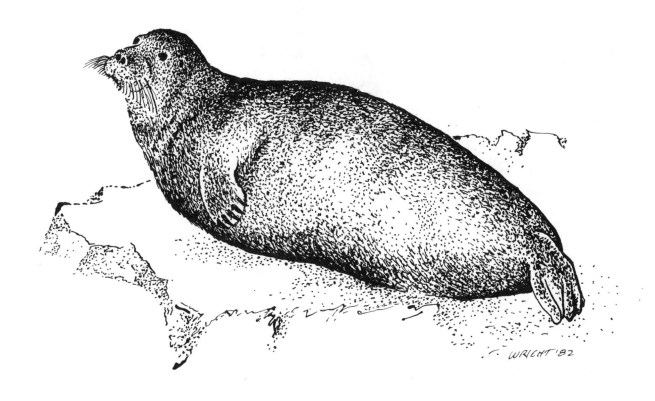

Distribution and Abundance

The bearded seal, although far fewer in number, shares its circumpolar habitat with the ringed seal. In Canada they occur in James Bay and along the Labrador coast are most abundant in Ungava Bay and north Hudson Bay. In Labrador they are often seen in spring coastal pack ice in the Hopedale, Nain and Hebron regions. Bearded seals live closely associated with shallow water sea ice year round. In many areas they are quite sedentary and make only local movements in response to ice conditions. In other areas they are migratory and follow the seasonal advance and retreat of ice cover. A crude population estimate for the Canadian Arctic is about 180,000 animals.

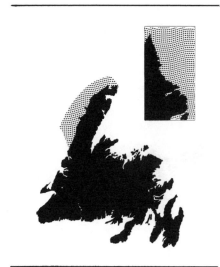

Polar bear

Natural History

The social organization of bearded seals is not well known. Pupping occurs on the ice from late April to the beginning of May. At birth pups are over 4 ft. long (1.2m) and weigh about 70 lbs. (32 kg). During the nursing period of 12-18 days they grow to nearly 200 lbs. (90 kg) and develop an adult fur coat

Bearded seals are sexually mature by 5-7 years and may live for up to 30 years. It is assumed that once mature they are annual breeders. Mating occurs from mid-April to mid-May. After breeding, development of the embryo is delayed for about 2.5 months; gestation lasts about 11.5 months ensuring births at about the same time each year.

Like walrus, bearded seals are bottom feeders using their snouts and flippers to capture clams, crabs and shrimp. Their breathing holes in the ice are clawed open using their muddy front flippers and are unique because of the bottom soil frozen around the opening.

Bearded seals are hunted by polar bears and man and are important to the Inuit as a dependable meat and hide source. However, only low numbers are harvested. One of the problems which occur in hunting bearded seals is that they are generally less buoyant than other arctic seals and tend to sink when killed. They are also difficult to stalk on ice but their underwater songs provide good location signals to kayaking hunters.

Walrus *(Odobenus rosmarus rosmarus)*

Identification

- rare in Newfoundland and Labrador waters
- hard to mistake for any other seal
- very large — heavy-bodied — 8-10 ft. (2.5-3m) weighing 1,200-2,000 lbs. (550-900 kg)
- males larger than females
- head short and square with a bushy moustache of stiff yellow bristles
- long yellowish tusks present in both sexes
- cinnamon-brown fur, short and sparse
- hair loss is common in older animals giving them a pale colour
- adult males often have many whitish scars, bumps and knobs on neck and body
- normally very sociable — almost always feed, travel or rest in groups
- lone sightings tend to be males

Identification of dead animals

- most positive traits are size — presence of tusks

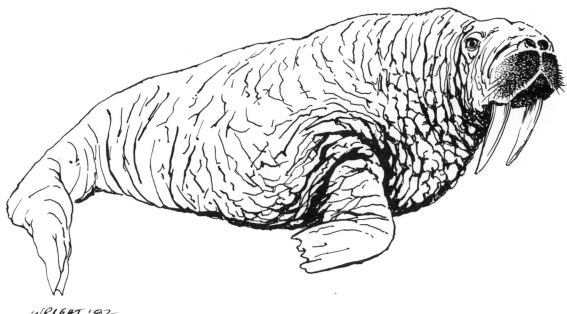

WRIGHT '82

Distribution and Abundance

Walrus are found in a circumpolar range above latitude 60 degrees north. Although found in arctic waters of both the Atlantic and Pacific Oceans about 80 percent of the estimated world population of 250,000 are found in the North Pacific. Numbers in the Canadian Arctic are poorly known. Walrus range from Ellesmere Island to the Okak Bay region of Labrador. They seem to wander on occasion or become lost, as extralimital sightings are fairly numerous — they have been seen as far south as Maine. Sightings in Labrador occur infrequently in the Okak region, between Hopedale and Button Islands and also near Nain. Occasionally they are reported in Newfoundland.

Natural History

Calves are born in April and weigh about 120 lbs. (55 kg). They are often seen clinging to their mothers' backs. Calves may be weaned after a year or may remain with their mother for a full two years. Most males become sexually mature between 6-7 years. Maturity in females is more variable, from 5-11 years, but most become sexually active by 8 years. The breeding season is from December through June. Normally females calve every three years. Walrus up to 28 years of age are possible; the oldest animal reported was 33 years old.

Tusks are modified canine teeth of the upper jaw. They appear during the first year and grow continuously. Tusks 40 in. (102 cm) long and weighing 12 lbs. (5.5 kg) have been recorded. They are used in courtship displays, for feeding and when hauling out on ice floes.

Walrus prefer a habitat of moving pack-ice on top of shallow water feeding grounds. They feed mostly on clams, diving to depths of 30-250 ft. (10-80 m). To locate their prey, they move their tusks from side to side along the bottom and then dig with the snout, much like a rooting pig. They can eat 3,000 clams in a single day.

Walrus have few predators other than humans. Young or sick animals may fall prey to polar bears or orcas, but the exceptionally ferocious adults are seldom molested.

In the 1950s-60s the annual take of walrus in Canada's Arctic was from 500-1,200 animals. Reliable hunting data for the 1970s is not available but some Arctic communities still hunt walrus irregularly.

Glossary

Bait: Specific food species of an animal. When in large quantities the bait will lure or draw predators into an area; eg. capelin is bait for many whales, fish and seabirds.

Baleen: (Whalebone) The cornified, fibrous plates attached to the upper jaws of certain whales for filtering food organisms from the sea water.

Basking shark: (Cetorhinus maximus) A plankton feeding shark common in some areas of Newfoundland. Feeds by swimming through the water with its mouth open, straining plankton from the water. The second largest fish in the world; lengths from 20-36 ft. (8-11 m) have been reported in Newfoundland waters.

Beak: Pointed, protruding snout or rostrum. Found on all dolphins.

Blubber: The dense, insulative fat of marine mammals deposited next to the skin. Commonly blubber was used as a source of oil.

Breach: The act of throwing the body out of the water, into the air. Humpbacks and white-sided dolpins are well known for their breaching.

By-catch: Animals that are caught accidentally or unintentionally by fishermen, although they are not the primary species for which the boat is fishing.

Callosities: Specific to right whales. Wart-like, light colored growths on the upper jaw. The pattern of callosities is unique to individuals and therefore allows observers to identify individual whales by photographs.

Carnivore: A meat-eating organism that preys or feeds on other animals.

Census: A count of the number of members of a population. Various sampling methods may be used such as aerial, shipboard or land sightings. By counting animals in a known sample area and time, an estimate of total populations can be made.

Cetacea: The mammalian taxonomic order containing the whales, porpoises and dolphins.

Circumpolar: Around, or on all sides of the polar region.

Cod-worm: (Phocanema decipiens) A nematode or roundworm, parasitic in marine creatures

Conservation: Management of a renewable resource in order to prevent waste and to maintain continuing populations.

Copulation: The act of sexual union or intercourse between males and females.

Crustacean: Any of a large class of arthropods, mostly aquatic and commonly covered with a hard, chitinous shell. Examples include lobsters, shrimp, crabs, barnacles.

Cryptic: Hidden, secret, camoflaged. Many animals rely on cryptic coloration to hide from their predators.

Delayed implantation: Suspended development of an embryo common in seals. It is a condition in which the fertilized egg ceases development for a period until the mother's hormonal level changes and then embryo growth continues. This allows all female seals to give birth at about the same time of year. This enables them to birth when environmental conditions are optimal and to have a short breeding season.

Diurnal: During the day, day-time.

Dolphin: A cetacean 8-12 feet long, with an external beak and sharp, conical teeth.

Dorsal fin: Finned appendage found on the back of some whales. It probably functions to guide the animal precisely through the water. In some species, such as killer whales, the difference in dorsal fins betweem males and females, suggest that it may have signal value. Some species of whales can be individually recognized by the shape and coloration pattern on and around the dorsal fin. Most species of whales have a species typical dorsal fin shape and placement which can aid in recognizing them.

Drive fishery: In several areas of the world, whales that live in groups are fished by herding or driving them to shore. This herding is very much like the process of herding sheep. Because of the social cohesiveness of the groups, animals do not scatter but continue to shore, where the group is killed.

Echolocation: Orientation by the use of echos of emitted sounds. Some animals, such as bats and whales, produce pulsed sounds. When these sounds hit an object, part of the sound energy is reflected back to the animal. This echo enables the animal to locate objects.

Ecology: The branch of biology dealing with the relationship between living organisms and their environment.

Endangered species: A species of animals where future survival of the group is threatened by habitat changes or excessive reduction of numbers in the population.

Euphausiids: Shrimp-like, planktonic crustacea.

Exploit: To utilize for one's own advantage or profit. Exploitation of wild animals involves the killing or harvesting of individuals in the population for one's own use or for commercial purposes.

Extinction: The disappearance of a species forever. When all animals of a given species are gone, the species is extinct. While extinction of species is a normal biological process, recently the rates have increased markedly due to the activities of man.

Extralimital: Outside of the usual area or known limits of that species.

Fathom: A measurement of 6 ft. (1.8m) usually of depths of water. Roughly approximated as the length of a man's arms outstretched, from fingertip to fingertip.

Flipper: The broad, flat forelimb of cetacea and pinnipeds, adapted for swimming.

Flippering: The act of waving a flipper in the air. Humpbacks are rather commonly seen flippering.

Fluke: The horizontal tail fin or appendage of a cetacean.

The Front: An oceanic area, north of Newfoundland and southeast of Labrador where harp seals congregate in spring.

Gestation: Pregnancy. The process in mammals of carrying young in the uterus.

Gregarious: Highly social, tending to herd or school together; habitually living or moving in a group.

Haul-out: Specific to seals when they climb out of the water onto ice or land. When a seal comes out of the water, it's said to be hauling out. The location where it comes out of water is called a haul-out.

Harem: A type of social and breeding organization where a group of females is associated with a single male.

Hierarchy: A social rank or order of individuals where each animal is subordinate to the one above it.

Ice: Land-fast ice: heavy ice that is frozen to the shore
   Pack ice: heavy ice that comes from the Arctic. Each spring pack ice comes into the Gulf of St. Lawrence and on to the Newfoundland and Labrador coasts.

Ice entrapment: A condition where, because of their need to regularly surface to breath, whales are confined to small areas of water (called polonyas). On occasion, animals will even be trapped against shore as the ice moves to the land.

Kayak: A small boat of the Inuit. Traditionally this was a sealskin covered boat propelled with a double-bladed paddle.

Krill: Small, shrimp-like crustacea that occur in huge blooms in cold ocean regions. Food for many marine organisms.

Lactation: The secretion of milk by the mammary gland of females.

Landsmen: Seal hunters based on shore using small boats and nets or rifles to hunt seals.

Larva: The immature, wingless and often worm-like form in which certain creatures hatch from the egg stage.

Leads: Openings or channels of open water in an ice-covered area.

Lee: A spot protected from the wind or weather.

Lob-tailing: The act of raising the flukes out of the water and then striking the surface of the water. Common in several species of whales.

Longevity: Length of life or lifespan.

Lunge feeding: Once a baleen whale has located a school of bait it will frequently dive underneath the school and push them against the surface. It then swims up, through the school with its mouth open. The whale is observed breaking through the surface of the water, frequently with its mouth still open and water streaming out of the sides of its mouth.

Management: The action of controlling and directing the conservation and harvesting of a resource to ensure continual regeneration and supply.

Mass strandings: Whales, especially toothed whales that live in close social groups, sometimes come to shore in groups. There are a number of possible explanations for such strandings, none wholly satisfactory.

Migration: The movement of animals from one area to another with the changing seasons.

Monogamous: A mating organization where one male breeds with only one female, during a mating season, or for life.

Moult: The process of shedding feathers or fur annually to renew

Moult: The process of shedding feathers or fur annually to renew and repair the worn outer covering.

Muktuk: An Inuit word for the skin and thin layer of blubber that is cut from marine mammals and used as food.

Mysticeti: Scientific name meaning baleen whales.

Navel: A depression in the abdomen where the umbilical cord from the mother was attached to the fetus. Commonly the navel is used as a reference point in measuring whales.

Odontocetes: Scientific name for all toothed whales.

Pinniped: Fin-footed mammals. The taxonomic order pinniped includes walrus, sea lions and seals.

Plankton: Small or microscopic plants and animals that drift passively with the currents and wind in the upper layers of the sea. Phytoplankton is the name for plant plankton. Zooplankton is the name for animal plankton.

Plankton bloom: A sudden, seasonal abundance of plankton.

Pod: A number of animals of the same species clustered together in an interrelated social group.

Polygamous: A mating organization where one male breeds with several females during the same season.

Porpoise: Cetaceans 4-8 ft. long, with no external beak-like jaw, and small, spade-shaped teeth.

Predator: An organism which lives by consuming other organisms.

Prey: What is hunted or killed by organisms (predators) for food.

Promiscuous: A mating system where an animal mates with several members of the opposite sex.

Quota: In a managed population, estimates are made of the number of animals that can be removed by harvesting. This portion is called the total allowable catch (T.A.C.). A quota is the portion of the T.A.C. that may be taken.

Range: Most animals have very specific, habitual areas in which they live. Suitability of areas is determined by the animals' basic needs for warmth, food, etc. The region which provides such basics and where the animal can be normally found is called the range.

Saddle: Coloration or markings or a ridge on the back of an animal suggestive of the round shape of a riding saddle.

Skimming: Method of feeding by certain baleen whales where they swim through the surface water with their mouths open, straining plankton from the water.

Sexual dimorphism: A difference in size or structure between males and females of the same species.

Social organization: Most animal groups have a definite order to the relations between members. Social organization refers to the way animals in a group relate to one another.

Sonar: A process by which sound is used to orient to objects. Usually high frequency sound is transmitted; when it strikes an object, some of the energy is reflected back (an echo) making it possible to locate the object.

Sound spectograph: Sonagram, a special graph to show what sounds look like.

Spy-hop: A common behaviour in some whales where they raise the head and eyes out of the water to look about.

Stock: A specific sub-group of an animal population; usually geographically separate.

Terminal dive: Final dive at the end of a series of blows at the surface. The terminal dive directly precedes the longest of a series of dives.

Territorial: The control and defensive behavior exhibited in a specifically defined area of land or water.

Total allowable catch (T.A.C.): The total catch on any species which may be allowed, based on scientific data about the size and productivity of a population.

Ventral grooves: Grooves or channels on the underside of the throat and belly of some baleen whales. These grooves allow expansion and permit the animal to engulf a large volume of water.

Vestigial pelvic bones: Tiny, left-over hind leg bones inside the bodies of a few whales. They no longer serve any purpose.

Weaning: To gradually restrict and finally stop provision of mothers milk to a young animal.

Whelping: To give birth; pupping.

Barnes, W.M., *When Ships were Ships and not Tin Pots: The Seafaring Adventures of Captain William Morris Barnes*. Edited by Hilda Renbold Wartman. Albert and Charles Boni Inc., N.Y., 1930. Anecdotes of a delightful, humorous, down-to-earth Newfoundland sailing captain.

Brice-Bennett, Carol, *Overview of occurrence of cetaceans along N. Labrador Coast*. OLABS Program Report, 1978, St. John's, Nfld.

Brower, Kenneth, *Wake of the Whale*. E.P. Dutton, New York, 1979. Beautiful photographs of whales by W.R. Curtsinger. Interesting text about diving and photographing whales.

Brown, Cassie, *Death on the ice; The great Newfoundland sealing disaster of 1914*. Doubleday Canada Ltd., Toronto, 1972. Informative and exciting historical narrative.

Chapskii, K.K. and V.E. Sokolov (editors), *Mythology and Ecology of Marine Mammals, Seals, Dolphins, Porpoises*. J. Wiley, New York, 1973.

Coish, Calvin, *Season of the Seal: the International Storm over Canada's Seal Hunt*. Breakwater Books, St. John's, Nfld. 1979.

Connolly, Joe, *On the front*. Jesperson Printing Ltd., St. John's, Nfld. 1978. Cartoons and caricatures of the seal hunt.

Decks Awash, "The Seal Hunt." Vol. 7, No. 1, Extension Service, Memorial University of Newfoundland, February 1978.

Doyle, Gerald S., *Old-time Songs and Poetry of Newfoundland*. G.S. Doyle, St. John's, Newfoundland, 5th Edition, 1978. Sealing, whaling and fishing songs of Newfoundland. "It is a well known fact that there is often more interesting history in the songs of a country, than its formal political records and state documents."

Engel, Leonard, *The Sea*. Time Life Books, New York, 1973. Good popular introduction to oceanography and marine biology. Well illustrated.

Gaskin, D.E., *The ecology of Whales and Dolphins*. Heinemann, London, 1982. A comprehensive, technical review for sophisticated readers.

Gosner, Kenneth L., *A Field Guide to the Atlantic Seashore*. Peterson Field Guide Series 24, Houghton Mifflin Co., Boston, 1978. Clear, concise guide to seashore, flora and fauna of Newfoundland area.

Graves, William, "The Imperiled Giants." *National Geographic*, Dec. 1976.

Howell, A.B., *Aquatic Mammals*. Charles C. Thomas, Springfield, Ill., 1930. A non-technical discussion of how marine mammals are adapted to aquatic life.

Jennings, Gary, "Newfoundland Trusts in the Sea." *National Geographic*, Jan. 1974.

Katona, S., V. Rough, and D.T. Richardson, *A Field Guide to the Whales, Porpoises and Seals of the Gulf of Maine and Eastern Canada, Cape Cod to Newfoundland*. Illustrations by John R. Quinn, D.D. Tyler, and Sarah Landry. Charles Scribner's Sons, New York, 1983. Comprehensive guide. Excellent text.

Kellogg, Remington, *Whales, Giants of the Sea*. Thirty-one paintings by Else Bostelmann, Washington, D.C., National Geographic Society, 1940.

Kellog, W.N., *Porpoises and Sonar*. University of Chicago Press, 1961. A popular book on the bottlenose dolphin.

Leatherwood, S., D.K. Caldwell and H.E. Winn, *Dolphins and Porpoises of the Western North Atlantic; A Guide to their Identification*. NOAA, National Marine Fisheries Service, Technical Report CIRC-396, Seattle, 1976. An excellent guidebook. Available from the U.S. Government Printing Office, Washington, D.C. Stock No. 003-020-00119-0.

Leatherwood, S., and Randall Reeves, paintings by Larry Foster, *The Sierra Club Handbook of Whales and Dolphins*. Sierra Club Books, San Francisco, 1983. Excellent field guide covering all cetacea species.

LeMessurier, Sally Lou, *The Fishery of Newfoundland and Labrador*, edited by Susan Sherk. Extension Services, Memorial University of Newfoundland, St. John's, Nfld., 1980. Well laid-out, good overall view of the fishery.

Lien, J. and Bora Merdsoy, "The Humpback is not over the Hump." *Natural History*, June 1979, pp. 46-49.

Lilly, J.C., *Lilly on Dolphins: Humans of the Sea*, Anchor Press, Garden City, NY, 1975.

Mathews, Leonard Harrison, *The Whale*. Crescent Books, NY, 1975. Coffee table book on species, whaling, history, and whale biology.

Mathews, Leonard Harrison, *The Natural History of the Whale*. London, Weidenfeld and Nicolson, 1978. World naturalist series. Plates and illustrations.

McIntyre, Joan, *Mind in the Waters*. Scribners, NY, 1974. On whales, dolphins, and animal intelligence. Collection of articles, poetry, excerpts.

Melville, H., *Moby Dick*, 1851. Various publishers. Much information on whales and whaling techniques.

Mercer, M.C., prints by David Blackwood, *The Seal Hunt*. Information Branch, Fisheries and Marine Service, Dept. of Fisheries, Ottawa, 1977. Factual, beautifully illustrated.

Mitchell, E. (editor) "Review of Biology and Fisheries for Smaller Cetaceans," *Journal of the Fisheries Research Board of Canada*, Vol. 32, No. 7, 1975.

Mowat, Farley, *A Whale for the Killing*. McClelland and Stewart, Toronto, 1972. Story of a fin whale trapped in an outport harbour in Newfoundland.

Mowat, Farley, *Wake of the Great Sealers*. McClelland and Stewart, Toronto, 1973.

Putnam, George Palmer, *Mariner of the North, The Life of Captain Bob Bartlett*. Duel, Sloan, and Pearce, NY, 1947. Newfoundland-born sea captain, good natural history on sealing, walrus, and descriptions of exploratory voyages.

Ridgeway, S.H. (editor), *Mammals of the Sea: Biology and Medicine*. Charles C. Thomas, Springfield, Ill., 1972. A general review of marine mammal biology.

Ridgeway, S.H., and Richard J. Harrison (editors), *Handbook of Marine Mammals*, Vols. 1 and 2, Academic Press, London, 1981. Excellent technical work, with scientific descriptions of all species of seals, sealions, and the walrus.

Scheffer, V.B., *The Year of the Whale*. Charles Scribner's Sons, NY, 1969. General descriptions of migration, diseases, food, senses, measurements of intelligence, and reproduction.

Scheffer, V.B., *A Natural History of Marine Mammals*. Charles Scribners' Sons, NY, 1976.

Slipjer, E.J., *Whales and Dolphins*. University of Michigan Press, Ann Arbor, 1976. A good basic book on whales; technical, but largely understandable by the layman. Chapters on evolution, history, behaviour, feeding, reproduction, distribution and the future of whales and whaling.

Whiteley, George, *Northern Seas, Hardy Sailors*. W.W. Norton and Co., NY, 1982. Informative and entertaining, with great photos of Newfoundland and Labrador. Covers sealing, bird-life, history, geology, and folklore.

Winn, H.E. and B.L. Olla (editors), *Behavior of Marine Animals, Current Perspectives in Research*, Vol. 3, *Cetaceans*. Plenum Publishing Corp., NY, 1979. Technical articles written by specialists in the field cover various aspects of whale behaviour.

Whale Books for Children

Broger, Achim. *Good Morning Whale*. Macmillan Press 1975.

Davidson, Margaret. *Nine True Dolphin Stories*. Hastings Press (hard cover), Scholastic Press (soft cover) 1974.

Goudey, Alice. *Here Come the Dolphins*. Scribners 1961: 94 pp. *Here Come The Whales*. Scribners 1956: 94 pp.

Griggs, Tamar, *There's A Sound In The Sea...A Child's Eye View Of The Whale.* Scrimshaw Press, San Francisco, 1975.

McGovern, Ann. *Little Whale.* Fourwinds Press, New York, 1979. A good story about humpbacks.

Renouf, Miriam and Bora Merdsoy, *A Whale By The Tail.* Jesperson Press, St. John's, Nfld., 1982.
Young, Jim, *When the Whale Came to My Town.* Knopf, 1974.

Suggested Teacher's Aids

Getting Along: Fish, Whales, and Fishermen. Grade 5 curriculum. The Whale Research Group, Memorial University, St. John's. Newfoundland Department of Education. Published by Breakwater Books, St. John's, 1984. Excellent, informative activity-oriented unit dealing with marine education, and the fishermen-whale conflict.

Men and Seals: The Story of Newfoundland's Sealing Industry. Multimedia Kit. The History and Social Science Council of Nfld., Centre for Audio-visual Education, Memorial University and GLC Educational Materials and Services Ltd., Nfld., 1973. Filmstrip of the seal hunt, first-hand interviews on tapes, and documents including logs, maps, newspaper articles. High school level (Gr. 7 and up).

The Seal and Labrador Cod Fisheries of Newfoundland. Shannon Ryan, Canada's Visual History. Vol. 26. National Museum of Man, and National Film Board of Canada. Text and slides very good, high school level.

Fisheries and Oceans, *Underwater World Series.* Excellent, up-to-date factual pamphlets on most Atlantic species of marine mammals, fish and shellfish, and some on marine issues.

Fisheries and Oceans, *Whale-Watching.* Pamphlet on guidelines to follow when whale-watching.

Posters on whales, sea birds, fish species and boats, available at Children's World, The Murray Premises, Water St., St. John's.

Films

And God Created the Great Whales. 27:50, colour, NFB. Killer whales filmed in the wild and captivity.

Beluga Days: 14:52, colour, NFB. Whale hunting down lower St. Lawrence River.

Down to the Sea. 29:35, colour, NFB. Marine scientists doing research on ocean ecology.

Fishermen. 21:43, B & W, NFB. A Day in the Life of an East Coast Fisherman.

ETV Research Series *How Not to Catch a Whale*, 30:00, colour. Memorial University of Newfoundland, St. John's, Nfld.

Life of Our Land Series: Features of the Newfoundland Environment Cassette 4, *The Sea*, Government of Newfoundland. Audio Tape Catalogue 1979.

Oceans of Science. 26:27, colour, NFB. Fisheries science film on restoring and protecting marine life.

The Harp Seal. 28:00, colour. Available from Newfoundland Department of Education film library. Natural history of harp seals and commentary on northern peoples' management of seal hunt.

Seal Hunting — Landsmen in 1973 and 1978. 17:00. B & W, Memorial University Extension Services. Shooting and hauling seals from small boats and shore.

The Sea. 28:36, colour, NFB. Scientific documentary of Canadian oceanographic vessel.

The Whales Are Waiting. 27:42, colour. NFB. Shows the two sides of whaling: whales as a food source vs. extinction.

Whale of a Tangle. 30:00, BBC. *Land and Sea* I and II. Cassette, 1980.

N.B. All *Land and Sea* TV programs are available from A-V Division, Newfoundland Department of Education.

Acknowledgements

We would like to thank Hal Whitehead, Nan Hennessey, Heidi Oberheide, Dong Jin Hai, Kate Bredin, Denis Chabot, Kathy Lynch, Peter McLeod and Heather Walters in the Whale Research Group at Memorial University and Don Bowen, Keith Hay, and Dave Sergeant of Fisheries and Oceans Canada for encouragement and help in preparing this guide.

We are also indebted to the reviewers: Hal Whitehead, Lindy Weilgart, Deane Renouf, Bill Montivecchi, and Tom Arnbom who provided criticisms and suggestions which have improved our initial efforts greatly. During the writing, our work has been supported by Fisheries and Oceans Canada, the Newfoundland Department of Fisheries, M.U.N. Extension Services and the Green Island Foundation and we gratefully acknowledge their support. The Department of Psychology and the Newfoundland Institute for Cold Ocean Science also aided us in many ways. We are especially indebted to the late Van Allen Clark for his guidance and interest in our work.

There are three groups of people who deserve special acknowledgement. An initial guide to whales of Newfoundland and Labrador was prepared for Canadian Coast Guard lighthouse keepers and M.U.N. "Whale Watchers" who regularly report sightings to us. Because of their reaction to the initial guide we were encouraged to launch the present effort.

We are profoundly grateful to those sea captains, sealers, whalers, merchants and scientists of Newfoundland and Labrador who, for centuries, have fished and observed marine mammals off our shores. They have established in Newfoundland tradition and culture a powerful respect for the sea, and for the whales and seals that live there. They have continually intrigued us with their stories and whetted our appetites to learn more of these wonderful animals.

The third group consists of a large number of fishermen in Newfoundland and Labrador with whom we have worked, attempting to alleviate the effects of the whale problem in the inshore fishery. Assaulted for the past decade by seal protest groups and incurring serious losses financially to whales, this group of men have endured the trouble and constructively worked for realistic solutions. The need to understand more of the whales and seals of Newfoundland and Labrador, on their behalf, provided our motivation in producing this book. With respect and admiration we dedicate it to them.

Local Contact Groups

Gros Morne National Park, P.O. Box 130, Rocky Harbour, Nfld. A0K 2L0. Whale interpretation programs, whale watching.

Harbour Charters; Boat Tours, Charlie Anonsen - Skipper. 22 Pilot's Hill, St. John's.

The Newfoundland Museum, Duckworth Street, St. John's, Nfld. A1C 1G9. Marine and whale displays including pilot whale skeleton, minke whale skull, and marine mammal displays.

Ocean Contact Ltd., P.O. Box 10, Trinity, Trinity Bay, Nfld. A0C 2S0. Whale watching tours by boat.

Terra Nova National Park, Glovertown, Nfld. A0G 2L0. Marine interpretation programs for the public and specifically for school groups, whale program, whale watching.

Whale Research Group, Memorial University, St. John's, Nfld. A1B 3X9. Can provide films, posters, fact sheets, and give talks on whale biology, behavior, and the entrapment problem.

Canadian Sealers Association, Cormack Building, 2 Steers Cove, St. John's. Helpful and informative.

Fisheries and Oceans Canada, Communications Branch, Building 302, Pleasantville. Can supply fact sheets, posters, films and information on fisheries resources and marine phenomena.